Mostly Plants

Also by the Pollan Family  *The Pollan Family Table*

Mostly Plants

101 Delicious Flexitarian Recipes
from the Pollan Family

Tracy, Dana, Lori & Corky Pollan

Foreword by **Michael Pollan**

Photographs by **Nicole Franzen**

HARPER WAVE

An Imprint of HarperCollinsPublishers

MOSTLY PLANTS. Copyright © 2019 by Old Harvest Way, LLC. Foreword copyright © 2019 by Michael Pollan. All rights reserved. Printed in the United States of America. No part of this book may be used or reproduced in any manner whatsoever without written permission except in the case of brief quotations embodied in critical articles and reviews. For information, address HarperCollins Publishers, 195 Broadway, New York, NY 10007.

HarperCollins books may be purchased for educational, business, or sales promotional use. For information, please e-mail the Special Markets Department at SPsales@harpercollins.com.

FIRST EDITION

Photographs by Nicole Franzen

Library of Congress Cataloging-in-Publication Data has been applied for.

ISBN 978-0-06-282138-6

19 20 21 22 23   LSC   10 9 8 7 6 5 4 3 2 1

For Stephen, husband and dad

Contents

Foreword

"Mostly plants," the two simple words that make up the title of this wonderful book, might just be the two most controversial words I've ever joined together. When I was laboring to distill into a single memorable phrase the best available wisdom on the healthiest approach to eating—"Eat food, not too much, mostly plants"—I had no idea how many people would get worked up over a modest little adverb. Carnivores were upset I had dissed their favorite food by failing to even mention it, while vegans and vegetarians were incensed that by qualifying plants with "mostly" I was being mealy-mouthed or, well, chicken: *why not* only *plants?* they insisted. Apparently in America these days, you have to be all in, on one side or the other, in our eating as in everything else.

But I recommended "mostly plants" because that is what the science tells us. We Americans tend to cast our eating choices in either-or ideological terms, and there is certainly environmental and ethical cases to be made for going vegetarian: meat eating contributes mightily to climate change, and many people question the morality of eating animals. It doesn't have to be that way—there are farms that raise animals sustainably and humanely, but these are still the exception to the rule of industrial meat production, and even at its most sustainable, a meat-centric diet has a bigger carbon footprint than a plant-based diet.

But the case I was making by advocating for a diet consisting mostly of plants was foremost about our health. Meat is undeniably a nutritious food, one that our species has been eating for as long as it's been a species; there is no good health reason to eliminate it entirely from the diet. Yes, the evidence for the benefits of a plant-based diet is as strong as any evidence the field of nutrition science has produced. But it's not like a little meat is going to kill you. A *lot* of meat, however, is another story, and that's what most of us eat every day—much to the detriment of our health, not to mention the health of the planet.

How did we get to a point where Americans eat on average more than half a pound of meat per person per day, many including it in every meal? Status is one reason: since meat is usually more precious than vegetables, being in a position to eat lots of it has always implied a certain social standing. Yet thanks to the efficiencies (and brutality) of industrial meat production, this luxury has been democratized, turned into a staple of fast food. Add to this that meat is dense with essential nutrients; it's usually easy and convenient to prepare; and for many of us it can be delicious.

I suspect the appeal of meat in our culture also owes something to the fact that, at least in the Anglo-American culinary tradition, vegetables have been so badly mistreated. Most of us grew up thinking a normal dinner consisted of a big chunk of animal protein in the middle of the plate, with a starch and a veg playing supporting roles—aptly called "sides." The starch was usually okay, but, truth be told, the quality of those vegetables—which often came out of a can or off a truck, tuckered out after a cross-country ride—didn't exactly deserve equal billing. All too often they were cooked badly and for way too long. No wonder they have always played second fiddle to meat in the American diet.

But all that is changing today, as the recipes in *Mostly Plants* so seductively demonstrate. The quality and diversity of vegetables in the typical American supermarket are better now than ever before. Fresh organic produce is available just about everywhere—even at Wal-Mart and Target! And the explosion in the number of farmers' markets has put the astonishing flavors of just-picked and field-ripened vegetables in reach of just about everyone. Also in the past few years, we have learned how to cook vegetables in ways that make the most of what they have to offer, in flavor and texture and sheer beauty. There has never been a better time to cook with vegetables—and to move plants to the center of the American plate. Even if plants weren't the better choice for your health, they make the case for themselves purely on the basis of deliciousness.

That is precisely the case made so convincingly by the recipes in this book: eat mostly plants because eating that way can be so satisfying when done well. And this book will teach you how to do it *very* well; several of the techniques on offer here manage to be both straightforward in execution and revelatory in result. (I'm thinking, for example, of roasting hardy vegetables on a sheet pan with nothing more than a spritz of olive oil and a sprinkle of sea salt, pepper, and an herb.) In recent years, American chefs and home cooks have exploded our sense of the possible when it comes to cooking with plants; this book brims with the excitement of all those possibilities.

Yet *Mostly Plants* is as reasonable and realistic as that adverb implies: don't let the gorgeous photos fool you, this is a cookbook that is firmly grounded in the real world, the one where most of us live and cook and eat. And the fact is, absolutism about eating is not how most of us really live, especially when we're trying to satisfy a wide diversity of eaters and appetites. There's something here for everyone, including the intermittent carnivore.

There's no good nutritional reason to banish meat from your table, not if you crave it or like what it can add to a dish. The research shows that vegetarians are healthier and longer-lived than the rest of us, but it also shows that "flexitarians"—those who eat meat once or twice a week—fare just as well as vegetarians. (Curiously, researchers can't say for sure whether the problem with a meat-centric diet is with the meat itself, or is it with the absence of the vegetables—and their healthful qualities—which all that meat pushes off the plate. But either way, the advice is the same: eat more plants, less flesh.)

Of course the flexitarian idea is not a new one: in many of the world's great peasant cuisines meat has always been used sparingly and strategically, for the rich flavors it can impart to vegetables, and *Mostly Plants* draws liberally on those great culinary traditions, too. The fact is, if you approach meat as a flavoring rather than a centerpiece, you can more likely afford to buy the kind of sustainably and humanely produced meat that you can enjoy with a clear conscience.

This book is not dourly anti-meat; rather, it is ecstatically pro-plant. Prepare to be inspired.

—Michael Pollan, author of *The Omnivore's Dilemma*
and *In Defense of Food*

Mostly Plants

Introduction

"Eat food, not too much, mostly plants."

With these seven simple words, Michael Pollan, our brother and son, started a national conversation about how we should eat for both optimal health and the health of the planet.

Eating mostly plants has revolutionized the way the four of us cook and eat. We find ourselves excited to plan meals around vegetables, while incorporating lean proteins and whole grains for flavor, texture, and satiety. For us, eating right is not about following the rules of a "diet"—rather, the key to healthy eating is choosing good-quality foods, lots of vegetables, whole foods, and home-cooked meals whenever possible. In this book, we will show you how to follow our "non-diet" diet. Our plant-centric recipes are not only good for keeping the body healthy and lean and the mind sharp, they're also highly doable (many of them can be thrown together in 35 minutes or less!) and delicious.

This may not come as a surprise, but it's worth mentioning that eating mostly plants is really good for you. When you focus on eating more vegetables, you naturally eat less meat and fewer processed foods. It's not about going completely plant-based or vegan (unless you want to). If you love meat or feel deprived without it, you don't need to give it up—you can simply change the ratio on your plate, using meat as an accent rather than a centerpiece. The diet-and-nutrition bookshelf is full of absolutists, fanatics, and idealists telling us what to do. Lecturing at us. We often feel that what's missing is a dose of realism—a recognition that for most of us, those black-and-white rules are impractical and give short shrift to flavor and pleasure.

We believe that the key to eating well, both for our own health and that of the environment, is not to overturn the dinner table, but simply to change its balance.

Each of us approaches this balance a bit differently. We grew up eating the classic American dinner, consisting of a meat centerpiece, a starch, a vegetable, and a salad—though often that salad was a wedge of iceberg lettuce slathered in Russian dressing and sprinkled with bacon bits. The way we eat now has evolved dramatically from those early family meals. What do our dinners look like today? Maybe soup and a salad, other nights it's a couple of sides, and sometimes we want to sit down to a big hearty bowl of chili and rice. Of the four of us, Corky eats the most meat, going vegetarian twice a week. Tracy goes vegetarian three to four times a week, and Dana and Lori go meatless every night. Our book is about being practical, realistic, and inclusive—you will find recipes that satisfy everyone, with helpful substitutions for those who are vegetarian, vegan, dairy-free, or gluten-free. And what's more, our dishes fulfill the need for meals that are as great tasting as they are nutritious. We've discovered that eating mostly plants is both intensely satisfying and delicious once you've mastered a few essential recipes and kitchen skills, and we hope to share what we've learned with you.

All of us can remember a time when cooking this way presented its challenges—you often had to visit several different stores just to find the right ingredients. But today every grocery store sells fresh herbs. Target offers organic produce. Spices can be ordered online for delivery to your doorstep. There's also been an

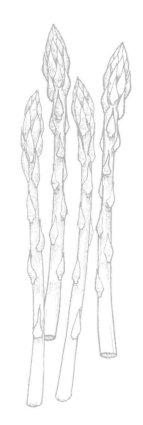

explosion of new grains and legumes that weren't previously available—think of the variety of lentils, or farro, or quinoa offered at your local grocery store. There's never been a better or easier time to create delicious, plant-based meals than right now.

Plants are Mother Nature's prescription for improved health. They are chock-full of protective vitamins, minerals, and antioxidants, many of which cannot be found in animal protein. We have long known that vegetarians are healthier than meat-eaters. The great news is, you don't have to give up meat completely to reap the benefits of a plant-based diet. In fact, there is compelling evidence that just cutting back on meat reduces the risk of many chronic diseases and can help you live longer.

According to a recent study, "Replacing 3 percent of dietary protein from animal products with proteins from grains, vegetables or other plants reduces the risk of death regardless of any other unhealthy lifestyle choice . . ."[*] Research shows that flexitarians are at a decreased risk for type 2 diabetes, have a reduced risk of many types of cancers and heart disease, have improved cholesterol levels, and in general have lower mortality rates from these diseases. In addition, studies have demonstrated that people who consume a plant-based diet also consume more of every essential nutrient the body needs, dispelling the myth that meat-free diets are nutrient deficient. As Michael has put it, "Vegetarians are healthier than carnivores, but near vegetarians ('flexitarians') are as healthy as vegetarians."[†]

Another bonus of eating mostly plants is that you will very likely lower your body mass index, lose extra pounds, and keep them off. Flexitarians weigh 15 percent less on average than their carnivorous counterparts. And of course, there's the bonus that far transcends the number on the scale: eating a plant-based diet also benefits our planet. Eating less meat slashes greenhouse gases; protects our water supplies, rivers, and oceans; and improves our food resources.[‡] What we put on our plates has a considerable effect on our own carbon footprints. In fact, abstaining

---

[*] https://www.upi.com/Health_News/2016/08/01/Increased-plant-protein-in-diet-reduces-risk-of-death-study-says/9501470067005/.

[†] http://www.nytimes.com/2007/01/28/magazine/28nutritionism.t.html.

[‡] http://www.davidsuzuki.org/blogs/science-matters/2016/05/eating-less-meat-will-reduce-earths-heat/.

from meat even just one day a week can make a significant difference for the environment—if everyone in the United States went vegetarian just for one day, we would save 100 billion gallons of water.*

So now down to the nitty-gritty: How does one eat a flexitarian, or *mostly* plant-based, diet? Do you need to go to the bookstore and buy a slew of new cookbooks? Follow a prescribed eating plan? Scroll through blogs and websites for recipes and rules? The answer is no—you don't need a different cookbook for every dietary choice. Everything you need is right here in your hands. In the pages to come you'll find a mix of vegetarian, vegan, dairy-free, and gluten-free recipes, as well as dishes that feature seafood, poultry, and meat. There are four of us, we all eat differently, and this book satisfies all our culinary desires—deliciously.

This book answers the question, "How do I make a nutritious meal that doesn't scream 'healthy' and that will put me on the road to a happier, more balanced lifestyle?" Our well-tested, much-beloved recipes offer everything you need to create delicious, nutritious, nourishing meals for you and your family. We will guide you to a healthier you, one great dish at a time.

* http://planetsave.com/2009/04/06/why-going-vegetarian-for-one-day-will-help-stop-global-warming/.

The Pollan Family Table

Our mom, Corky, is a wonderful cook. When we were young, she made the most incredible family meals. There was almost always some type of meat on the table, so we all grew up eating meat pretty regularly. Over time, we've each developed different tastes and personal philosophies about how we eat. Three of us have been vegetarians at some point in our lives, and two of us still are. For the other two, meat is a part of a flexitarian lifestyle. With that in mind, we wanted to share a little bit about how we eat and live individually, so you can better understand where we're coming from with our recipes and our approach to food.

Dana

Without sounding too spiritual, I believe I was destined *not* to eat meat. When I was young, I *loved* meat. Give me a steak, roast beef, brisket, bacon . . . You name it—I ate it. And then, when I was nine years old, my father decided to surprise us all and brought home a pet baby pig for my brother, Michael. Her name was Kosher. We nurtured her and fed her milk from a baby bottle, and she slept in a makeshift bed in one of Michael's dresser drawers. Kosher became a part of our family. Suffice it to say, as I grew older, it became exceedingly difficult for me to eat meat and not think about what, or rather *whom*, I was eating.

While it was Kosher's arrival that triggered my internal moral struggle, the first time I actually heard the term "vegetarian" was from my sisters. Tracy decided to become one on a whim, thanks to an article she read in *Seventeen*. Her refusal to eat meat at family meals made me consider what I was consuming in a way I never had before. Like so many other kids who have sensitivities to texture, for me, eating meat brought a physical discomfort, like accidentally biting into a fatty piece of beef and then chewing for what felt like an eternity. Now, with eyes opened wide by my sisters to this new way of eating, I realized not only that I didn't like consuming meat, but that *I no longer had to*. So when I was sixteen years old, I made the decision to give up meat.

Back then vegetarianism was an unusual dietary choice. Restaurants seldom had a vegetarian option. Eating out usually meant a plate of steamed vegetables. Plain. Beans and legumes were rarely on menus, and tofu was not yet popular in the United States.

People I'd come in contact with expressed their concern that a meatless diet would negatively impact my health. They would ask, *If you don't eat meat, what do you eat? How can you possibly get enough protein?* My answer for both: cheese, peanut butter, and lots of vegetables. Of course, the perception of vegetarianism has changed dramatically, with research consistently supporting all of its health benefits.

Today, I live in a household of flexitarians. My husband and sons eat meat, but not nearly as much as I did growing up. The one exception is my daughter. Like me, at sixteen, she became a vegetarian. I guess the two of us were destined *not* to eat meat.

Tracy

I have to admit that growing up, I was a die-hard carnivore. Given the choice between my mom's roast beef with Yorkshire pudding and just about any other dinner, nine times out of ten, the cow won (or I guess, in this case, I should say lost). This was how I ate for the first fifteen years of my life. Then something happened: my monthly copy of *Seventeen* came in the mail, and as I was poring through it I came upon an article singing the praises of the vegetarian diet. I decided immediately that I was now a vegetarian. Excited to share my news, I ran into the kitchen to tell my mother, who was substantially less enthusiastic about this decision. To her credit, she accepted it but said that she absolutely would not prepare a separate meal for me; I could eat the vegetables and sides that she served with the main course, and that would have to suffice. Her determination lasted maybe two dinners, and pretty soon she was whipping up dishes just for me. Using a cornucopia of vegetables along with cheese and beans, she created vegetarian meals that were as tantalizing as her heartiest steak dinners.

I remained vegetarian for the next twenty years. I was a vegetarian throughout my first pregnancy and gave birth to a very healthy eight-and-a-half-pound baby boy. It wasn't until my second pregnancy (with twins) that I began to think about eating meat. What started as a simple craving became a ravenous desire that my husband likened to a wolf taking down a deer at full speed. It felt as if my body was telling me that I simply couldn't consume enough protein and iron to feed not only me but also the two growing babies inside me. Slowly I began to reintroduce meat into my diet.

Now I would describe myself as flexitarian. Of the five or so nights a week I cook dinner at home, usually three or four of those meals are completely vegetarian, and the others are mostly plant-based with a small portion of meat. I still sometimes cook red meat, and I definitely enjoy going out to a steak dinner for special occasions. This allows me the freedom to experiment with my cooking and to try new things. For myself and my family, this is the diet that works best.

Lori

I believe that if you ask twenty vegetarians how they practice vegetarianism, you will get twenty different answers. In my experience, there is a broad vegetarian spectrum. I'm not sure where I fall on that spectrum, but I am motivated by the choices that work best for me.

I first became a vegetarian when I was thirteen years old. I remember it well—we were driving to Martha's Vineyard for a vacation when I took a big bite into a gristly roast beef sandwich. That was it—no more meat for me. I continued like this for about a year; however, I didn't know much about what constituted a healthy vegetarian diet, so I just ate around the meat at family meals. The end result was a doctor's checkup that showed slight anemia and the admonition that I add some meat to my diet, which I promptly heeded. I didn't love it, but at the time it seemed like my best option.

Five years later, at college and knowing better how to incorporate iron-rich foods and non-meat proteins into my diet, I stopped eating meat for good. Living in Northern California made vegetarianism easy—there was abundant produce, awareness of the healthy benefits of eating plenty of legumes and whole grains, and greater access to vegetarian menu options. When I think back to my motivation then, it wasn't purely environmental, ecological, or political—I just didn't like the taste or sensation of eating meat. I felt healthier, lighter, and more energetic without it. By degrees, the humane and environmental factors began to figure more and more profoundly for me.

Today I would perhaps call myself a "flexitarian ovo-lacto vegetarian"—I eat (and love) dairy and eggs, but I don't eat any meat or fish. That being said, although my preference is to avoid any meat products whenever possible—I check labels, no chicken stock in my soup, no gelatin-filled gummies or marshmallows, no lard in my refried beans—I will eat Parmesan and other cheeses that contain rennet when that's all that's available.

These days, having been vegetarian for what feels like eons, I do my best without being too inflexible or stringent—I've learned how to make my vegetarian diet a little easier for myself and for others. If I'm invited over to friends' homes for dinner, I'll forewarn them that I don't eat either meat or fish, but insist that they don't go out of their way to make something special for me—that I'm happy with sides and salads. Or when I watch a counterperson use the same knife to cut my veggie sandwich that was just used for a meat one, I might cringe a little, but at this point in life I try to let it go.

Corky

I grew up in the forties in a family of four, with two older brothers and a sister eighteen months younger than me. Of the four of us, I was the child who especially loved meat. I was such a carnivore that when my mom served a roast beef or leg of lamb, she couldn't leave the platter of meat on the table, or I would consume it all.

I loved just about everything my mom cooked, from the fried herring for Sunday brunch to the offal (sweetbreads and tongue) she sometimes made to the roast duck she cooked on special occasions. Oddly enough, though I had such a craving for beef, I loved vegetables, too, so much so that whenever my family went to a restaurant for dinner, I invariably ordered the vegetable plate.

Since I was the best eater, my mom would often ask me to help plan our menus, a job I loved. I would go with her to the local butcher shop and choose the cuts of beef she would cook over the next couple of days, making sure my favorites were included.

Our family dinners were classic for the times: a protein (beef, lamb, or chicken), a starch (usually potatoes), and a vegetable. Carrots, peas, or string beans (often canned) were the ubiquitous vegetables served at most family tables, but my mom would cook fresh asparagus, artichokes, and broccoli. These vegetables were quite unusual in those days, but since my father was in the produce business, they were often on our dinner table.

When my children were little, I pretty much duplicated the dinners I had as a child, but as the kids grew older—and with two vegetarians in the family—I made sure there were plenty of vegetables on our plates, and much less meat than I'd had as a child.

Around the time I turned fifty, I suddenly experienced a dramatic change in my eating habits, and I no longer craved red meat. I can remember so clearly the last burger I ate. I had been yearning for one and stopped into one of those Hamburger Heaven spots in New York City. I took one bite, and immediately knew that it would be my last. It just tasted too beefy. Years later I had the same experience with lamb. Rack of lamb was once a favorite, my go-to restaurant dish, but one summer on Martha's Vineyard I had pasture-raised lamb, and the flavor was way too intense for me. I've rarely eaten beef or lamb since. Pork has supplanted beef in my culinary affections, and I've discovered the infinite variety of poultry and the unlimited possibilities of seafood and fish.

Though I never thought of becoming a vegetarian, I love Meatless Monday meals so much that they often extend to a few other days of the week. After consuming one of these dinners, I'm sated but don't feel heavy or stuffed; instead I feel a surprising lightness, which I love.

CHAPTER 1

How to Use This Book

"...it's easy to open this book any day of the week..."

This book is not focused on what you need to *remove* from your diet, meat or otherwise. We want to focus on what you can *add* to it: more healthy whole grains, beans, and fresh produce.

The key to a flexitarian way of life is literally being flexible about how you eat and choosing what works best for you and your family. There's no one way or right way to do this. If you want a steak or a burger, go for it, then maybe double up on your greens the next day. If a meal doesn't feel complete without some animal protein, try to choose healthier proteins and use smaller portions. Some people find it helpful to follow a schedule where they go meatless one, two, or three days a week. Or go vegetarian except for your mother's turkey on Thanksgiving. And of course, like Dana and Lori, you can choose to go meatless every day.

In this book you will find recipes that fit all of these lifestyle choices. Many dishes are vegetarian. In most of the dishes that do contain animal protein, the ratio of meat, poultry, or fish is about 40/60 to vegetables, whole grains, and legumes: recipes like our Vegetable-Loaded Turkey Chili (page 90), Dry-Fried Beef with Vegetables (page 196), and Asian Parchment Parcels with Salmon or Tofu (page 164). We also offer more traditional meat-centric plates where we use smaller portions of meat, and always include plenty of vegetables. So it's easy to open this book any day of the week and select a recipe that appeals to the way you want to eat that night.

Special Features: Guiding You to Cooking Success

Look for these icons on each recipe:

Vegetarian	Vegan	Dairy-Free	Gluten-Free	Fast
🥗	◎	⊘	GF	⏱

With each recipe there is a symbol that denotes whether the dish is vegetarian, vegan, dairy-free, and/or gluten-free. Included are adjustments you can make to the recipes to accommodate these dietary needs. In addition, there is an icon that indicates whether a recipe can be prepared in 35 minutes or less, which is a lifesaver for hectic weeknight meals.

For people with serious food allergies or celiac disease, it is imperative to read all labels on any packaged or processed foods. Oftentimes, manufacturers will change ingredients on products that were once acceptable for your diet. In addition, ingredients can vary from brand to brand.

For those who follow a gluten-free diet, some store-bought chicken and vegetable broths contain gluten, while others don't—the same holds true for blended spice mixtures and some condiments. You can easily modify any of our pasta recipes by substituting a gluten-free noodle.

Our vegetarian recipes are ovo-lacto and often contain dairy and eggs. Vegetarians should be aware that some cheeses have rennet. Whether this matters to you is an individual choice, so feel free to substitute a rennet-free cheese when applicable.

MARKET AND PANTRY LISTS

Every recipe has a Market and Pantry list with a breakdown of all the ingredients you will need to prepare that dish. We suggest using your phone to take a photo of the list—it makes grocery shopping a breeze. Market ingredients are grouped by department (Produce, Dairy, Grocery, etc.). The ingredients in the pantry lists are the ones we suggest you keep on your shelves for a well-stocked pantry (see page 23 for our full pantry list).

OTHER FEATURES

We find that being prepared is the key to triumph in the kitchen, so we offer a number of additional features in this book with the intention of guiding you to culinary success. Our "Indispensable Utensils" (page 25) are the kitchen tools we use on a regular basis. They not only make life easier in the kitchen—they also sharpen your cooking skills. In "Sage Advice and Thyme-Tested Shortcuts" (page 26), we share our favorite hacks, techniques, and time-savers. "Tips to Make Any Dish Taste Better" (page 29) offers culinary pointers to help you troubleshoot or simply enhance your dish, so you achieve great flavor balance every time you cook. Interspersed throughout the recipes you will often find boxes titled "Food for Thought," which provide information about the health benefits of ingredients. Things just seem to taste better when you know that they're better for you!

Guide to Choosing Produce, Seafood, Poultry, and Meat

Local, organic, conventional, wild-caught, free-range: There are so many labels on our food these days that it can be daunting to know what to choose. What's more, the landscape is constantly changing—for example, a fish that is deemed sustainable today may be classified as overfished tomorrow. And labels such as "cage-free" or "free-range" don't guarantee that chickens are raised humanely.

So how best to navigate all these options? The first step is to understand the facts behind the labels so we can make informed decisions. We do this not only for our own health but also because we care about the lives of the animals we eat and the environment we inhabit.

We have put together some guidelines and resources to help you become a more conscious consumer.

PRODUCE

In an ideal world, we would buy all our fresh fruits and vegetables either from a local farmer's market or from the organic section of the supermarket. However, organic produce is more expensive than conventional, and that can be prohibitive to family food budgets. We have learned that it is important to know when buying organic is necessary and when it is not. The Environmental Working Group (EWG) is a wonderful resource for this information. It publishes a yearly list of fruits and vegetables with the highest pesticide residues called the Dirty Dozen, as well as those with the lowest pesticide residues, the Clean 15. The EWG's list can help you decide when it is essential to go organic—say, when purchasing strawberries or spinach—and where you can safely save your money with vegetables that have a lesser toxic load, such as avocados and asparagus. For a complete list, check out the EWG's website at https://www.ewg.org/foodnews/.

It all comes down to need, choice, and availability. When possible, we always prefer to shop at our local farmer's market or farm stand. We know that we are getting produce that is in season and at the peak of freshness. We find that a menu basically creates itself when we are presented with a cornucopia of heirloom tomatoes or luscious baby summer squash. Another resource we find ourselves returning to again and again is Local Harvest (https://www.localharvest.org/farmers-markets/). This website can direct you to both local farmer's markets and CSAs (community-supported agriculture) in your neighborhood. When it comes to buying organic, local, or conventional produce, we don't have any hard-and-fast rules; we do our research so we can make conscious, educated choices.

DAIRY

When it comes to dairy products, particularly milk, butter, and yogurt, our first choice is always grass-fed. Grass-feeding cows improves the quality of their milk—it is richer in omega-3 fatty acids, beta-carotene, and CLA (an extremely heart-healthy fatty acid). When grass-fed dairy is not available, we opt for organic or local, which have many of the same health benefits as grass-fed.

When possible, we avoid dairy products from conventionally raised cows because these animals are often injected with synthetic growth hormones. What's more, the animals are generally raised in inhumane conditions and in a manner more damaging to the environment.

SEAFOOD

Understanding how to make the best choices for seafood purchases is becoming more challenging every day, as the health of our oceans is in constant peril. Which fish contain the least mercury? Which are the most sustainable (i.e., harvested in a way that doesn't harm other sea creatures or damage the ecosystem)? There is no universal labeling system—like there is for chicken, beef, and dairy—to guide us when purchasing seafood, so it's up to us, as consumers, to collect as much information as we can to make educated choices.

Fortunately, there are many helpful resources, like the Monterey Bay Aquarium's Seafood Watch website and app (http://www.seafoodwatch.org/). Here consumers can find up-to-date lists on local seafood classified as "best choices" and "good alternatives," as well as the fish to "avoid." The site also has a "super green list." These classifications provide information on fish "that [have] been caught or farmed in environmentally responsible ways" *and* suggest the healthiest options—those low in mercury and packed with omega-3s. The Marine Stewardship Council (https://www.msc.org/), a nonprofit organization, is another invaluable resource. It has set criteria for what makes a wild fishery sustainable. The MSC certification and label is the most accepted sustainable label for wild-caught seafood.

Although more expensive, wild-caught is typically a healthier option than farmed fish, which can contain more bacteria, pesticides, and parasites. These fish are often given antibiotics and artificial dyes to help maintain their color. A caveat: Larger wild-caught fish, like swordfish and tuna, accumulate the most toxins since they eat lots of smaller fish, and therefore have higher mercury levels. Not to mention that the methods for catching these fish can harm the ocean habitat and cause overfishing. In this case, sustainably farmed fish may actually be the better choice. Smaller fish generally accumulate fewer contaminants and, in turn, are healthier.

POULTRY AND EGGS

Deciding what kind of poultry or eggs to buy at the market can be completely bewildering. If your primary concern is selecting a healthy and/or more humanely raised product, food labels might not be of much assistance.

Many of the words that appear on the packaging of eggs and poultry are simply marketing terms. Don't be misled by claims such as "natural" (which means no artificial ingredients), "hormone-free" (the FDA requires that all poultry are raised without hormones), or "farm-raised" (that farm can be a factory farm).

Other terms are more helpful for making sound choices but still are not absolutely clear-cut: antibiotic-free, free-range (depending on the farm, the poultry may actually have limited access to outside space), and organic (which, by definition, must be both antibiotic-free and free-range, and no pesticides or chemical fertilizers can be used in the poultry feed). Organic eggs are healthier for us as consumers, but take into consideration that the organic rules can be inexact and don't necessarily mean that the farming conditions are more humane than for conventionally raised birds.

The classifications that have the most definitive significance in terms of humanely farmed poultry are Certified Animal Welfare Approved by A Greener World (AGW) and Certified Humane Raised & Handled. Bear in mind that poultry with these designations are often more expensive.

When it comes to buying eggs, the above information also holds true. Organic, pasture-raised, and free-range, although not quantifiably regulated, are a step in the right direction.

Ultimately, for many people, the choice is economic; organic and local farm-raised poultry and eggs are generally more expensive. For us, selecting humanely raised, local, and/or organic when it comes to poultry and eggs is a financial tradeoff we make whenever possible.

Here are a few more tips for purchasing and handling poultry and eggs:

1. To find farmers selling poultry and eggs in your area, check out LocalHarvest.org or EatWild.com.

2. Don't wash your poultry—it can increase the risk of cross-contamination. Instead, blot it with clean paper towels if necessary.

3. Always thaw frozen poultry in the refrigerator.

4. A pink color in cooked poultry doesn't necessarily mean it's undercooked—the best indicator of doneness is an internal temperature of at least 165°F.

5. When it comes to eggs, a vegetarian label means that the hens are not fed animal protein, *but* since hens love to eat bugs and worms, this label can mean the hens aren't let outside to forage.

6. White and brown eggs are no different nutritionally—eggshell color depends on the breed of hen.

7. The color of egg yolks is a product of the hens' healthier diet—not breed.

8. Store eggs in their carton in the main part of the refrigerator for freshness.

MEAT (BEEF, LAMB, AND PORK)

When you're shopping for meat at your neighborhood market, words matter more than the cut or color of the beef. USDA organic grass-fed beef was once the label to look for, but the government has recently revised the standard and it no longer means the animals have been fully pastured and eat only grass and forage (hay and legumes). Often the animals are "finished" on soy and corn to fatten them up, and they may end their days in a feedlot, thus nullifying any pasture-raised claims.

Cows are ruminants (animals that chew their cud) and are unable to digest the large amounts of grain they're fed in feedlots, so they're given antibiotics and chemical supplements. When we eat cows raised this way, we also consume trace elements of antibiotics, pesticides, and growth hormones. Grass-fed cattle, on the other hand, are never fed antibiotics or hormones. In addition, grass-fed beef is more nutritious than grain fed, leaner in fat content, and higher in antioxidants, omega-3 fatty acids, vitamin E, magnesium, and potassium.

Unfortunately, grass-fed beef is also more expensive than conventional beef. Yet when meat is used more as a side dish or a flavor—as it is in the recipes in this book—one or two pounds of beef can go a long way, producing dishes that easily serve four to six.

Here are the labels we look for when we want to know if the beef we're buying is 100% grass-fed and if the animals have been treated humanely: American Grassfed Association, Certified Grassfed by AGW, Food Alliance Grassfed, or PCO Certified 100% GrassFed.

Look to these labels when buying lamb, too. Sheep, like cows, are ruminants, and in factory farms sheep are fed grain and given antibiotics, pesticides, and hormones to help them process it. When sheep are grass-fed and allowed to graze, their meat is higher in omega-3 fatty acids, vitamin B12, and minerals than grain-fed lamb.

Unlike cows and sheep, pigs are omnivores and can eat everything, and in the factory farms where many pigs are raised, they're fed the dregs of the food chain and live in crowded and inhumane conditions. When buying pork, seek out meat from pasture-raised pigs that have eaten grasses and tubers, and dug and foraged. Their meat is leaner and healthier than meat from factory-raised pigs, and higher in vitamins and omega-3 fatty acids.

To find local farmers selling 100% grass-fed beef and lamb and pasture-raised pork in your area, go to EatWild.com.

The Pollan Pantry

A well-stocked pantry is the key to liberation in the kitchen. There's nothing more aggravating then getting halfway through a recipe only to realize you're missing a critical ingredient. We have discovered that when our pantry is filled with the essential ingredients we use on a regular basis, the entire cooking process is faster, easier, and more enjoyable. We have assembled a comprehensive list that includes our most-used and fundamental oils, vinegars, spices, condiments, and other ingredients. Our list is extensive; you don't need to buy everything at once. Choose the ones you will use most often first, then build your pantry gradually.

We buy organic varieties of these foods whenever possible. In particular, we stock our pantry with organic broths, beans and legumes (canned and dry), grains, and flours. There are a couple of items that we deem nonnegotiable: we only buy organic tofu, edamame, and canola oil, which are not made with genetically modified organisms (GMOs). Of course, the choice of whether and what to purchase organic is yours to make.

OILS

Canola oil, organic	Grapeseed oil	Peanut oil
Coconut oil	Olive oil cooking spray, organic	Toasted sesame oil
Extra-virgin olive oil		Vegetable oil

VINEGARS

Apple cider vinegar	Champagne vinegar	Sherry vinegar
Balsamic vinegar	Red wine vinegar	White vinegar
Balsamic vinegar glaze	Rice vinegar	White wine vinegar

DRIED HERBS AND SPICES

Bay leaves	Cinnamon, ground	Garlic powder
Black peppercorns, whole	Cloves, ground	Kosher salt
Cayenne pepper	Coriander, ground	Nutmeg, ground
Chili powder	Cumin, ground	Onion powder

Oregano, dried

Paprika: smoked and sweet

Red chile peppers, whole dried

Red pepper flakes, crushed

Sea salt

Turmeric, ground

White pepper, ground

THE CUPBOARD

All-purpose flour

Baking powder

Baking soda

Bread crumbs: plain, panko

Broth, organic, low-sodium: chicken and vegetable

Cornmeal

Cornstarch

Farro

Legumes, canned organic: black beans, cannellini

beans, kidney beans, navy beans, refried beans, chickpeas

Legumes, dried: chickpeas, French lentils, green lentils, green split peas, red lentils

Mirin

Nutritional yeast

Old-fashioned rolled oats

Pastas: regular, whole-grain, chickpea, lentil,

quinoa, per dietary needs and preferences

Quinoa

Rice: long-grain brown, long-grain white

Semisweet chocolate chips

Sriracha sauce

Tomatoes, canned: crushed, pureed, whole peeled

Tomato paste

Vanilla extract, pure

REFRIGERATOR

Asian fish sauce

Capers

Dijon mustard

Ketchup

Mayonnaise

Nuts, raw: pistachios, walnuts

Seeds, raw: sesame, shelled pumpkin seeds (pepitas)

Soy sauce, low-sodium

Tahini (sesame paste)

Tamari

White miso paste

Worcestershire sauce

SPIRITS

Red wine

Sherry, dry

Vermouth, dry

White wine, dry

SWEETENERS

Agave nectar

Honey

Maple syrup, pure

Sugars: brown (light and dark), confectioners', granulated, turbinado

Indispensable Utensils

We have found that in cooking our *Mostly Plants* recipes, there are certain kitchen tools that are indispensable. We have compiled a list of the utensils that will make your time in the kitchen a breeze.

12-inch stainless steel skillet with a lid

Cast-iron skillet

Chef's knife

Citrus press, manual or dome

Dutch oven

Fine-mesh strainer or sieve

Fish spatula (turner)

Food processor

French rolling pin

Immersion blender

Instant-read thermometer

Jars with lids (such as Mason jars)

Large grill pan

Large stockpot

Liquid measuring cups, especially 2- and 4-cup measures

Mallet or meat hammer

Mandoline

Measuring spoons, with an ⅛-teaspoon measure

Microplane

Nonstick skillet

Parchment paper

Paring knives

Pepper mill

Salad spinner

Salt cellar

Silicone basting/pastry brush

Spider skimmer

Spring-loaded tongs, metal and/or silicone-tipped

Steamer, bamboo or pot insert

Wire cooling rack

Y-shaped vegetable peeler

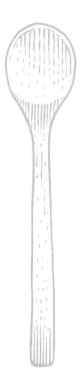

Sage Advice and Thyme-Tested Shortcuts

Over the years, the four of us have accumulated hard-won knowledge of how to save time in the kitchen and get the best results every time we cook. Here we share our favorite cooking how-tos, tips, and strategies.

- When cooking vegetables in oil, wait until the oil begins to shimmer before adding the vegetables to the pan.

- Always use a serrated knife when slicing tomatoes to cut through the soft skin without crushing the tomato.

- A quick and efficient way to slice leafy greens (think basil, spinach, kale) into fine strips is to chiffonade—stack the leaves, roll them tightly, then cut across the roll with a sharp knife.

- Cut down on the oil or butter you use by brushing it over the pan with a silicone brush.

- Annotate your recipes. If you change something and it works, write it down.

- Determine if an egg is fresh by placing it in a bowl of water. If it sinks, it's fresh; if it floats, it's old.

- Don't always live by the "sell by," "use by," and "best if used by" dates stamped on food products—these terms are standardized and at times meaningless. Focus instead on the smell, look, and taste to help you determine if a food is still good.

- When poaching eggs, strain each one in a sieve before cooking to remove the excess watery part of the egg. Your eggs will be more perfectly shaped.

- Use coarse salt for seasoning meat.

- Before serving a savory dish, add a sprinkling of salt to bring out its full flavor.

- Add a drizzle of good-quality olive oil to a finished dish for extra flavor.

- Keep guacamole green by gently pressing a piece of plastic wrap directly against its surface.

- When making soup stock, save prep time and add flavor by leaving the skin on the onions when you add them to the pot.

- Save Parmesan rinds to add flavor to a soup or stock.

- Peel fresh ginger using a spoon. To easily mince ginger, use a Microplane grater. Store knobs of fresh ginger in the freezer—they'll last longer and be easier to grate.

- Coat your cheese grater with nonstick cooking spray before grating—it'll make grating easier and cleanup quicker.

- Store fresh herbs properly to help them last longer. For tender herbs like parsley, mint, cilantro, and basil, trim the stems, place them in a jar or glass with cool water, and cover loosely with a plastic bag. Store all in the refrigerator except the basil, which should be stored on your kitchen counter. Change the water every few days. For hard herbs such as rosemary, thyme, sage, and chives, wrap them in a damp tea towel and place in a resealable plastic bag or container. Store in the vegetable drawer.

- Partially freeze fish or meat before slicing or dicing—this makes it easier to slice and to attain uniform pieces.

- To peel hard-boiled eggs more quickly, run them under cool water while peeling.

- No need to whisk vinaigrette salad dressing—just put the ingredients in a jar, seal the lid, and shake.

- Don't overcrowd your pan when sautéing or roasting—the ingredients will steam and get soggy instead of browning.

- When working in the kitchen, clogs or Crocs really save your back.

- Use a clean linen tea towel for drying greens and herbs instead of paper towels to save money and paper.

- Keep your knives sharp. You won't have to work as hard, and they'll do a better job of slicing the food. A sharp knife is actually safer to use than a dull one.

- To keep salad greens fresh, wrap washed and dried greens in tea towels and store them in either a plastic storage container or resealable plastic bag.

- When sautéing, if more oil is needed, add it by drizzling it around the outer edges of the pan. This way, the oil will be heated by the time it reaches the food being cooked.

- To ripen an avocado or mango more quickly, store it in a brown paper bag on the kitchen counter. For even quicker results, add a banana or apple to the bag—this will release ethylene gas, which speeds up the ripening process.

- When cooking grains, cook double the amount you need and store the leftovers in the refrigerator for quick weeknight meals (bowls, stir-fries, grain salads, etc.).

- To bring water to a boil more quickly, place a lid on the pot.

- Place peeled onions in a bowl of cold water for a few minutes before slicing to prevent your eyes from burning.

- If using more than one baking sheet when roasting, rotate the pans halfway through the cooking time, as ovens have some spots that are hotter than others.

- Keep a salt cellar on your counter; it's so much more convenient for salting.

- When making dough with butter, freeze the butter and then grate it into your flour.

- Store fresh garlic, dried herbs, and spices in a cool, dark place for the best flavor and longest shelf life.

- Make sure the bowl you're working with is big enough so that you can mix and incorporate all the ingredients thoroughly.

- Roll your dough between two sheets of parchment paper, lightly flouring the bottom sheet. This will cut down on the amount of flour you need, giving the dough more flavor and making it easier to work with.

- When baking, let your butter, milk, and eggs come to room temperature before you begin.

- Make sure lemons and limes are at room temperature before juicing; you'll get more liquid out of them.

- Save time by popping a fresh clove of garlic in a garlic press with the peel still on.

- Chop the whole bunch of parsley when it's called for in a recipe and freeze what you don't use for another day.

- Add woody, rich herbs such as thyme, oregano, and sage early in the cooking process and tender herbs like parsley, basil, and cilantro at the end.

- Toast nuts before adding them to any dish to heighten flavor. Roast or toast the entire package of nuts and store what you don't need in an airtight container.

- Toast grains (such as rice, quinoa, farro) before adding water to the pot to enhance their flavor.

- If a recipe calls for cooking pasta or blanching vegetables, bring a pot of water to a boil as soon as you start to cook, then reduce the heat to keep it at a simmer until ready to use.

- For an easier tomato sauce, grate fully ripe tomatoes on a box grater directly into your skillet or saucepan.

- If a recipe calls for lemon juice, squeeze the whole lemon, storing and refrigerating the remainder in a jar.

- When deep-frying, to determine if your oil is hot enough, insert the handle of a wooden spoon into the oil. If bubbles form around the wood and begin to float, the oil is ready.

- Freshly grind your black pepper.

Tips to Make Any Dish Taste Better

We've all been there. You've got a big pot of soup on the stove; you taste it and know something's missing. It's good but not great. Does it need more salt? A splash of vinegar? Or do you need to start all over again? Don't panic—there are myriad tried-and-true solutions. After many successes and mishaps in the kitchen, we've compiled a list of strategies to help boost the flavor of any dish. Sometimes it's the small touches that make a big difference in distinguishing a great dish from a so-so one.

When cooking mostly plant-based recipes, it is of utmost importance to strike the right balance of flavor. There are five basic universal tastes that we perceive on our taste buds: sweet, salty, sour, bitter, and umami (earthy/meaty). The best way to ensure that your dish has the right balance of flavor is to taste and adjust as you cook. Here are some of our go-to tips for striking that balance in any recipe:

Is your dish too sweet? Try adding:

- Acid—**citrus, white wine, or vinegar**
- Spice—**crushed red pepper flakes, hot sauce, or cayenne pepper**
- Salt—**soy sauce, tamari, or salt**

Is your dish too spicy? Try adding:

- Dairy/nondairy—**a dollop of sour cream, yogurt, or coconut milk**
- Acid—**lemon juice, lime juice, yuzu juice, or vinegar**
- Sweetener—**brown sugar, honey, or agave**

Is your dish too sour? Try adding:

- Sweetener—**carrots to a tomato sauce, brown sugar, honey, or agave**
- Salt—**soy sauce, tamari, or salt**

Umami

The fifth taste, umami, is thought to be the one that makes food more savory, satisfying, and deeply flavorful. It may sound counterintuitive, but adding this "meaty" flavor to mostly plant recipes is a game changer. It's important to add umami to all your savory dishes, but it is often challenging when cooking vegetarian and vegan meals. Be sure to stock some of these ingredients in your pantry so you can easily achieve that rich and full balance.

- Capers

- Miso

- Dried mushrooms—shiitake, porcini, cremini, etc.

- Sea vegetables such as kombu, kelp, and nori

- Nutritional yeast

- Olives

- Ume plum vinegar

- Toasted seeds and nuts

- Tomato paste and sun-dried tomatoes

- Chipotle chiles in adobo sauce

- Spices such as cumin, chili powder, smoked paprika, and curry powder

- Fermented foods such as soy sauce or tamari, amino acids, Worcestershire sauce*, kimchi, wine, beer, and balsamic vinegar

- Green tea

- Anchovies*

- Anchovy paste*

- Asian fish sauce*

* Non-vegetarian

CHAPTER 2

Meze and Bites

Crispy Parmesan Roasted Chickpeas

MAKES 3 CUPS   TIME: 25 MINUTES

These simple Parmesan chickpeas are so addictive that when we make them, our family and friends cannot stop eating them until the bowl is empty. And that's okay, because they are so nutritious. Only three ingredients (plus salt and pepper), and full of plant-based protein. Serve these as a snack, a party hors d'oeuvre, or in lieu of croutons on soups or salads.

2 tablespoons plus 2 teaspoons extra-virgin olive oil

Two 15-ounce cans chickpeas, drained, rinsed well, and patted dry, or 3 cups cooked chickpeas

½ cup firmly packed freshly grated Parmesan cheese (not pre-grated or it will not melt)

Sea salt

Freshly ground black pepper

1. Preheat the oven to 425°F.

2. Pour the 2 tablespoons of olive oil into a 4- or 5-quart baking dish (or divide the oil between two smaller baking dishes). Place in the preheated oven.

3. In a medium bowl, combine the chickpeas, the remaining 2 teaspoons olive oil, the Parmesan cheese, ½ teaspoon salt, and ⅛ teaspoon pepper. Mix well until the chickpeas are thoroughly coated.

4. Carefully remove the hot baking dish from the oven and pour the chickpea mixture into it.

Use a wooden spoon to spread the chickpeas into a single layer. Roast for 10 minutes, then stir with the wooden spoon and continue to roast until crispy and golden brown, an additional 7 to 9 minutes. Season with additional salt and pepper as desired, and serve hot or at room temperature.

DO NOT DRAIN THE CHICKPEAS ON PAPER TOWELS OR THEY WILL LOSE THEIR CRISPINESS.

Food for Thought

Chickpeas are ranked one of the healthiest foods for weight loss. One cup of these legumes provides 94 percent of the daily recommended intake of protein and 50 percent of fiber. The high amounts of protein and fiber in chickpeas help create a feeling of satiety, even while consuming fewer calories. Chickpeas are also high in iron, zinc, and B vitamins, especially folate.

From the Market
Parmesan cheese
(2 ounces, not pre-grated)

From the Pantry
Extra-virgin olive oil
(2 tablespoons plus
2 teaspoons)
Chickpeas (two 15-ounce cans
or 3 cups cooked)

Sea salt
Black pepper

Spiced Sweet Potato Crisps

2 TO 4 SERVINGS TIME: 50 MINUTES

Sliced very thinly and with just the addition of your favorite spice, these sweet potato crisps become a delectable, nutritious stand-in for higher-calorie potato chips. Serve them as a snack or with soups and sandwiches.

Organic olive oil cooking spray

1 large sweet potato, peeled and very thinly sliced (use a mandoline if you have one)

1 teaspoon seasoning of choice (such as paprika, smoked paprika, ground cumin, ground cinnamon, or chili powder, or a mix)

Sea salt

1. Set a rack in the middle of the oven and preheat the oven to 375°F. Lightly spray two rimmed baking sheets with the cooking spray.

2. Arrange the sweet potato rounds in a single layer on the baking sheets (taking care not to crowd or overlap them). Spray the tops with a fine mist of cooking spray and lightly sprinkle with your spice of choice (do not salt them yet, as this releases moisture).

3. Place one of the baking sheets in the oven on the middle rack and bake for 12 to 15 minutes, until the rounds are beginning to crisp at the edges. Flip the rounds, sprinkle with additional spice to taste, and rotate the pan in the oven. Bake until the rounds are lightly browned around the edges and tender in the middle, an additional 5 to 7 minutes. Watch them closely in the last 5 minutes, taking care not to let them burn; remove any rounds that have browned from the baking sheet and place them on a wire rack to continue crisping. Once the first batch is done, repeat with the second baking sheet. Season with salt and serve.

From the Market
Sweet potato (1 large or about 1 pound)

From the Pantry
Organic olive oil cooking spray
Spice(s), such as paprika, smoked paprika, ground cumin, ground cinnamon, and/or chili powder (1 teaspoon)

Sea salt

Perfect Kale Chips

4 SERVINGS TIME: 30 MINUTES

Our guilt-free kale chips are crisp, addictive, and healthy. We were weary of burnt or wilted kale, so we worked on this recipe to achieve perfection. The three keys to success: make sure your kale is completely dry, spread it in a single layer on the baking sheet, and do not salt until after it is done cooking. We enjoy these chips as snacks or hors d'oeuvres.

4 cups packed curly kale, completely dry, stemmed and torn into 2-inch pieces

1 tablespoon extra-virgin olive oil

Sea salt

1. Preheat the oven to 425°F. Line a rimmed baking sheet with parchment paper.

2. Place the kale in a large bowl and add the olive oil. Using your fingers, massage the oil thoroughly into the leaves (do not add salt yet, as it draws out moisture and the kale won't crisp).

3. Arrange the kale in a single layer on the prepared baking sheet. Roast until browned and crisp, about 15 minutes, flipping once halfway through. Season with salt and serve.

From the Market
Curly kale
(1 bunch or about 1 pound)

From the Pantry
Extra-virgin olive oil
(1 tablespoon)
Sea salt

*You will need parchment paper.

Buffalo Cauliflower

4 SERVINGS TIME: 35 MINUTES

Traditional Buffalo wings are deep-fried pieces of chicken doused with a spicy sauce that is very high in sodium. We make our vegetarian version using cauliflower and bake them, swapping out the hot sauce for harissa, which is not only more interesting but also is much lower in salt. These tasty bites are great as a crowd-pleasing appetizer or as a side.

¾ cup all-purpose flour

1 teaspoon garlic powder

1 teaspoon paprika

Kosher salt

Freshly ground black pepper

½ cup buttermilk

4 cups bite-size cauliflower florets

2 tablespoons unsalted butter

¼ cup harissa (mild or spicy)

Your favorite dip, such as a yogurt-based ranch dressing, for serving

1. Preheat the oven to 450°F. Line a rimmed baking sheet with parchment paper.

2. Place the flour, garlic powder, paprika, ½ teaspoon salt, and ⅛ teaspoon pepper in a medium bowl and whisk to combine. Stir in the buttermilk and ⅓ cup water and whisk until smooth. Place the cauliflower in the batter and toss to coat. One piece at a time, shake off the excess batter and lay the cauliflower florets in a single layer on the baking sheet. Leave enough space between them (about ½ inch) so the cauliflower does not get soggy.

3. Bake until crispy, 6 to 8 minutes. Flip the florets and bake until the other side is browned, an additional 6 to 8 minutes. Remove from the oven and set aside.

4. Reduce the oven temperature to 350°F.

5. Meanwhile, in a small saucepan over medium heat, melt the butter. Remove from the heat and pour into a medium bowl. Add the harissa and stir to combine. Add the cooked cauliflower and toss to coat evenly. Discard the parchment paper from the baking sheet and replace it with a fresh piece. Return the cauliflower to the baking sheet and bake for 10 to 15 minutes, flipping halfway through, until browned and crisp. Serve hot, with your choice of dip on the side.

From the Market
Cauliflower (1 small head)
Buttermilk (½ cup)
Unsalted butter (2 tablespoons)
Harissa, mild or spicy (¼ cup)

From the Pantry
All-purpose flour (¾ cup)
Garlic powder (1 teaspoon)
Paprika (1 teaspoon)
Kosher salt
Black pepper

*You will need parchment paper.

Vegan/Dairy-free: use unsweetened almond milk and vegan butter in place of buttermilk and butter.

Crispy Kimchi and Scallion Pancakes

4 TO 6 SERVINGS TIME: 40 MINUTES

We grew up eating Chinese take-out every Sunday night, and one of our staples was scallion pancakes. In updating this typically heavy, greasy classic, we add our go-to flavor booster, kimchi, to our version, and the end result is flaky, crispy perfection. These are wonderful both as an appetizer when entertaining or as a main with a side of greens.

FOR THE DIPPING SAUCE

2 tablespoons low-sodium soy sauce

2 tablespoons rice vinegar

¼ teaspoon toasted sesame oil

½ teaspoon granulated sugar

½ teaspoon chopped dried red chile pepper

1 teaspoon thinly sliced scallion

FOR THE PANCAKES

1 cup all-purpose flour

½ cup rice flour

Kosher salt

1 large egg, beaten

1 cup cold seltzer

¼ cup kimchi liquid
(reserved from draining the kimchi)

1 cup kimchi, drained and chopped

4 scallions, thinly sliced, green and white parts separated

1 tablespoon chopped fresh medium-spicy red chile pepper (such as Thai bird or cayenne)

3 to 4 tablespoons organic canola oil

FOR THE DIPPING SAUCE:

1. In a small bowl, combine the soy sauce, vinegar, sesame oil, sugar, dried chile pepper, and scallion with 2 tablespoons water and stir to combine. Set aside.

FOR THE PANCAKES:

2. Preheat the oven to 300°F.

3. In a large bowl, combine the two flours, ½ teaspoon salt, the egg, seltzer, and kimchi liquid and mix well to incorporate. Add the kimchi, scallion whites, and fresh red chile pepper and stir to combine.

4. In a large nonstick skillet over medium-high heat, heat ½ tablespoon of the canola oil until shimmering. Ladle about ½ cup of the batter into the pan and cook undisturbed until golden brown, 2 to 3 minutes. Flip the pancake and cook until the second side is golden brown, 2 to 3 minutes more. Transfer to a rimmed baking sheet and place in the oven to keep warm. Repeat with the remaining oil and batter, making six to eight 8-inch pancakes.

5. Remove the pancakes from the oven and slice into quarters. Garnish with the scallion greens and serve with the dipping sauce.

Continued

Food for Thought

Kimchi is low-calorie, low-fat, high-fiber, and nutritionally packed. It is a powerhouse of vitamins such as A, B1, and C, but its biggest benefit may be in its healthy bacteria called *Lactobacilli* (the same bacteria found in other fermented foods like yogurt). These good bacteria help with digestion, and some studies show that fermented cabbage has compounds that may prevent the growth of cancer.

From the Market

Kimchi (1 cup, plus ¼ cup liquid)

Scallions (5)

Fresh red chile pepper, such as Thai bird or cayenne (1)

Large egg (1)

Seltzer (1 cup)

Rice flour (½ cup)

From the Pantry

Low-sodium soy sauce (2 tablespoons)

Rice vinegar (2 tablespoons)

Toasted sesame oil (¼ teaspoon)

Granulated sugar (½ teaspoon)

Dried chile pepper (1)

All-purpose flour (1 cup)

Kosher salt

Organic canola oil (3 to 4 tablespoons)

Pesto and Parmesan Stuffed Mushrooms

8 TO 10 SERVINGS   TIME: 20 MINUTES

These pesto-stuffed mushrooms are the essence of simplicity and elegance. Four ingredients are quickly transformed into perfect little appetizers that finish cooking in less than 15 minutes.

Organic olive oil cooking spray

1 cup prepared basil pesto

½ cup freshly grated Parmesan cheese

2 tablespoons plain bread crumbs

24 medium cremini or button mushrooms, stemmed

Kosher salt

Freshly ground black pepper

1. Set a rack in the middle of the oven and preheat the oven to 375°F. Lightly spray a rimmed baking sheet with the cooking spray.

2. Combine the pesto, Parmesan cheese, and bread crumbs in a small bowl. Using a small spoon, stuff the mushrooms with the pesto mixture, about 2 teaspoons each, being careful not to overstuff them.

3. Arrange the mushrooms in a single layer on the prepared baking sheet. Season lightly with salt and pepper. Bake until golden brown, 8 to 10 minutes. Remove from the oven, let cool for 5 minutes, and serve.

From the Market

Cremini (baby bella) or button mushrooms (24 medium)

Basil pesto (1 cup)

Parmesan cheese (2 ounces)

From the Pantry

Plain bread crumbs (2 tablespoons)

Organic olive oil cooking spray

Kosher salt

Black pepper

Creamy Homemade Hummus

MAKES 1 QUART   TIME: 45 MINUTES PLUS OVERNIGHT

Once you make your own hummus it is almost impossible to go back to store-bought. It's actually quite simple, and you can refrigerate hummus for up to 5 days or freeze it for 6 to 8 months. There is nothing more irresistible than dipping a pita chip or a raw vegetable into this warm, creamy, garlicky homemade version.

1¼ cups dried chickpeas

1 teaspoon baking soda

¼ cup fresh lemon juice

3 cloves garlic, minced

Kosher salt

1 cup plus 2 tablespoons tahini (sesame paste)

½ teaspoon ground cumin

⅓ cup ice-cold water, plus more as needed

2 to 3 teaspoons extra-virgin olive oil

Paprika, for dusting

1. Place the chickpeas in a bowl and add cold water to cover by 3 inches. Soak overnight at room temperature.

2. Drain and rinse the chickpeas. Put them in a medium saucepan and add water to cover by 4 inches. Add the baking soda and bring the water to a boil. Reduce the heat to medium-high and simmer, skimming off the foam and any chickpea skins that float to the top, for about 30 minutes, or until the chickpeas are very tender, then drain them.

3. Meanwhile, in a food processor or high-speed blender, combine the lemon juice, garlic, and ½ teaspoon salt and let sit for 5 to 10 minutes.

4. Add the tahini, cumin, and 1 teaspoon salt and process until you have a thick paste, 1 to 2 minutes. With the motor running, slowly drizzle in the ice-cold water and process until smooth and creamy.

5. Add the drained chickpeas to the tahini mixture and process until very smooth and creamy, 2 to 3 minutes, adding more cold water as needed to reach your desired consistency.

6. Place the hummus in a serving bowl, drizzle with the olive oil, and dust with the paprika. Serve warm.

From the Market
Lemons (2)
Garlic (3 cloves)

From the Pantry
Dried chickpeas (1¼ cups)
Baking soda (1 teaspoon)
Kosher salt
Tahini (1 jar)

Ground cumin (½ teaspoon)
Extra-virgin olive oil
(2 to 3 teaspoons)
Paprika (for dusting)

CHAPTER 3

Salads

Mesclun Greens with Persimmons and Manchego Cheese

4 TO 6 SERVINGS   TIME: 20 MINUTES

We love adding fruit to our greens and are thrilled when persimmon season comes around. Known as "the fruit of the gods," persimmons are deliciously sweet with a delicate, honey-like flavor. We pair them here with toasted pistachios and salty Manchego cheese—the combination is scrumptious.

½ cup shelled pistachio nuts

Sea salt

3 tablespoons Champagne vinegar

1 tablespoon finely chopped shallot

1 teaspoon Dijon mustard

½ cup extra-virgin olive oil

Freshly ground black pepper

5 to 7 ounces mesclun greens

2 firm but ripe Fuyu persimmons, peeled, halved, and sliced into thin wedges (if not available, use 1 Bosc pear, halved lengthwise, cored, and thinly sliced)

½ cup shaved Manchego cheese

1. Preheat the oven to 350°F.

2. Spread the pistachio nuts in a single layer on a rimmed baking sheet. Bake until fragrant, 7 to 9 minutes. Transfer to a plate and set aside.

3. In a small bowl, stir together ¼ teaspoon salt, the vinegar, and the shallot. Let sit for 2 to 3 minutes to allow the shallot to mellow. Add the mustard, olive oil, and pepper to taste. Whisk until emulsified.

4. Place the mesclun and half the persimmon wedges in a large salad bowl. Pour on half the dressing and toss gently to coat. Add more dressing to taste and gently toss again. Place the greens and persimmon wedges on individual salad plates. Arrange the remaining persimmon wedges on each salad, sprinkle with the pistachio nuts and Manchego cheese, and serve.

From the Market

Fuyu persimmons (2) or if not available, use Bosc pear (1)

Mesclun greens (5 to 7 ounces)

Shallot (1 small)

Manchego cheese (3 ounces)

From the Pantry

Shelled pistachio nuts (½ cup or about 3 ounces)

Champagne vinegar (3 tablespoons)

Extra-virgin olive oil (½ cup)

Dijon mustard (1 teaspoon)

Sea salt

Black pepper

Vegan/Dairy-free: Omit the cheese.

Mango, Avocado, Tomato, and Watercress Salad

4 SERVINGS TIME: 20 MINUTES

During the hot summer months, there is nothing more refreshing than a fruit-focused salad. This one features a colorful, flavorful combination of sweet-tart mango, creamy avocado, luscious tomatoes, and peppery watercress. We finish it with Marcona almonds for a buttery, satisfying crunch.

FOR THE DRESSING

1 teaspoon minced shallot

1½ tablespoons Champagne vinegar

3 tablespoons grapeseed oil

Sea salt

Freshly ground black pepper

FOR THE SALAD

1 bunch watercress (thin stems and leaves only)

2 tomatoes, cut into ¼-inch-thick slices

1 ripe mango, peeled and cut into ¼-inch-thick slices

1 ripe avocado, cut into ¼-inch-thick slices

4 tablespoons roasted Marcona almonds (or any roasted blanched almonds)

1 tablespoon balsamic vinegar glaze

1 tablespoon chopped fresh basil

FOR THE DRESSING:

1. In a small bowl, whisk together the shallot and vinegar. Slowly add the grapeseed oil and whisk until completely emulsified. Add a pinch of salt and pepper to taste.

FOR THE SALAD:

2. Place the watercress in a bowl, add dressing to taste, and toss to coat. Arrange the slices of tomato on four individual salad plates. Mound the watercress on top of the tomatoes and then alternate slices of the mango and avocado on top of the watercress. Add 1 tablespoon of the almonds to each salad, drizzle with the balsamic vinegar glaze, and sprinkle with the basil. Season with salt and pepper and serve.

Food for Thought

Watercress is a true powerhouse vegetable—ranked number one in nutrient density with a score of 100 by the Centers for Disease Control and Prevention. Not only does watercress have prodigious amounts of vitamins C, K, and A, as well as calcium, it also has significant levels of compounds that have been shown to deactivate carcinogens and inhibit cancers.

From the Market

Watercress (1 bunch)

Tomatoes (2 medium)

Avocado (1 ripe)

Mango (1 ripe)

Shallot (1 small)

Fresh basil (1 small bunch)

Marcona almonds, roasted, or other roasted blanched almonds (¼ cup)

From the Pantry

Champagne vinegar (1½ tablespoons)

Grapeseed oil (3 tablespoons)

Sea salt

Black pepper

Balsamic vinegar glaze (1 tablespoon)

Asian Tofu Sesame Salad with Spinach

4 SERVINGS TIME: 20 MINUTES

For such a quick and easy salad, this one really packs a punch. The spice of the Thai bird chile pepper, the sweetness of the mirin, and the saltiness of the soy sauce all complement one another beautifully. We love to serve this salad with a simply prepared grilled piece of chicken or fish.

1 teaspoon sesame seeds

Kosher salt

8 ounces baby spinach

¼ cup low-sodium soy sauce

2 tablespoons plus 1 teaspoon mirin

1 tablespoon rice vinegar

2 teaspoons toasted sesame oil

½ teaspoon agave nectar

One 14-ounce package silken tofu, drained and gently dried and cut into 1-inch cubes

2 Persian or seedless cucumbers, thinly sliced

2 tablespoons chopped scallions

1 teaspoon minced fresh ginger

1 small fresh hot red chile pepper, such as Thai bird or cayenne, thinly sliced, or to taste

1. Set a small dry skillet over medium heat. Add the sesame seeds and shake the pan occasionally until they begin to brown, 3 to 4 minutes. Transfer to a small plate and set aside.

2. Fill a large bowl with water and ice and set aside.

3. Bring a large pot of water to a boil. Add 1 teaspoon salt. Place the spinach in the boiling water and once wilted, about 15 seconds, remove with a large slotted spoon and transfer to the ice water to stop the cooking. Place the spinach in a strainer and gently squeeze out any excess water. Once the spinach has cooled, place it on a tea towel and gently pat dry. Set aside.

4. In a small bowl, whisk together the soy sauce, mirin, vinegar, sesame oil, and agave.

5. Divide the spinach among four individual salad plates or bowls. Arrange the tofu, cucumbers, scallions, ginger, and chile pepper slices on each and sprinkle with the toasted sesame seeds. Spoon 2 tablespoons of the dressing over each salad and serve.

From the Market
Baby spinach
(8 ounces)
Persian or seedless cucumbers (2)
Fresh ginger (1 small knob)
Fresh hot red chile pepper, such as Thai bird or cayenne (1 small)
Scallions (2)

Silken organic tofu
(one 14-ounce package)

From the Pantry
Sesame seeds (1 teaspoon)
Kosher salt
Low-sodium soy sauce
(¼ cup)
Mirin (2 tablespoons plus 1 teaspoon)

Rice vinegar (1 tablespoon)
Toasted sesame oil (2 teaspoons)
Agave nectar (½ teaspoon)

Gluten-free: use tamari in place of soy sauce.

Watermelon, Feta, and Arugula Salad with Balsamic Glaze

6 SERVINGS   TIME: 15 MINUTES

In this savory salad we combine watermelon with salty feta cheese, which enhances the sweetness of the melon. We add sweet, peppery basil, and finish it off with a balsamic vinegar glaze. This is our new go-to summer salad—it's so refreshing on a hot day. Try mixing both yellow and red watermelon for an even more spectacular presentation.

4 ounces arugula

¼ seedless watermelon, rind removed, flesh cut into 1-inch cubes (about 3 cups)

One 8-ounce block good-quality feta cheese, cut into ½-inch cubes

⅓ cup sliced red onion, halved lengthwise and thinly cut into half-moons

¼ cup packed fresh basil leaves, very thinly sliced (see chiffonade, page 26)

3 tablespoons extra-virgin olive oil

1 tablespoon balsamic vinegar glaze

1 tablespoon balsamic vinegar

Sea salt

Freshly ground black pepper

Arrange the arugula on a serving platter. Top with the watermelon, then the feta cheese, then the onion. Sprinkle with the basil. Drizzle the olive oil over the salad, followed by the balsamic vinegar glaze, and then the balsamic vinegar. Season with ⅛ teaspoon salt and ⅛ teaspoon pepper and serve.

Food for Thought

Watermelon often gets a bad rap as being mostly water and loaded with sugar, when in fact it is packed with many nutrients, particularly vitamins A and C. Watermelon is one of the richest natural sources of citrulline, which, among other benefits, helps to lower blood pressure and reduce muscle soreness.

From the Market
Arugula (4 ounces)
Seedless watermelon (¼ whole or 3 cups cubed)
Red onion (1 small)
Fresh basil (1 bunch)

Feta cheese, good-quality (one 8-ounce block)

From the Pantry
Balsamic vinegar glaze (1 tablespoon)
Balsamic vinegar (1 tablespoon)

Extra-virgin olive oil (3 tablespoons)
Sea salt
Black pepper

Pear Carpaccio and Frisée Salad
with Walnut Vinaigrette

4 TO 6 SERVINGS   TIME: 20 MINUTES

Almost nothing beats the harmonious combination of fresh salad greens, tangy cheese, and fruit, and this particular medley is one of our favorites. The thinly sliced pear serves as an elegant base and goes perfectly with the slightly bitter flavor of the frisée. Walnuts provide the perfect crunch and a hint of earthiness.

¾ cup raw walnut halves

Organic olive oil cooking spray

Sea salt

2 tablespoons white wine vinegar

½ teaspoon Dijon mustard

2 teaspoons minced shallot

2 tablespoons walnut oil

2 tablespoons extra-virgin olive oil

3 ripe but firm red or yellow Bartlett pears

5 ounces baby arugula

3 ounces frisée (if not available, use 1 endive, cut into thin strips)

½ cup crumbled mild semi-firm blue cheese

Freshly ground black pepper

1. Preheat the oven to 350°F.

2. Spread the walnuts on a rimmed baking sheet. Lightly spray with the cooking spray (or toss with ½ teaspoon extra-virgin olive oil) and sprinkle with ⅛ teaspoon salt. Toast in the oven until they begin to brown and give off a nutty aroma, 8 to 10 minutes, stirring them once halfway through. Remove from the oven and set aside. Once cool, roughly chop them.

3. In a small bowl, whisk together the vinegar, mustard, and ⅛ teaspoon salt. Add the shallot. Slowly whisk in the walnut and olive oils. Set aside.

4. Using a sharp knife or mandoline, cut the pears lengthwise into ⅛-inch-thick slices. Slice one side of the pear, then the other, avoiding the core and seeds. Fan the pear slices around four to six individual salad plates. Drizzle the slices with about 1 teaspoon of the dressing per plate.

5. Place the arugula in a medium bowl. Add 3 tablespoons of the dressing and toss to coat. Arrange a pile of arugula in the middle of each plate. Place the frisée in the same bowl and toss with the remaining 1 tablespoon dressing. Scatter the frisée on top of the arugula. Sprinkle the cheese and nuts on top of each salad. Season with salt and pepper and serve.

From the Market

Bartlett pears, red or yellow (3 ripe, but firm)

Baby arugula (5 ounces)

Frisée (3 ounces) or if not available, use endive (1)

Shallot (1 small)

Semi-firm blue cheese (3 ounces)

Walnut oil (2 tablespoons)

From the Pantry

Raw walnut halves (¾ cup)

Organic olive oil cooking spray

Sea salt

White wine vinegar (2 tablespoons)

Dijon mustard (½ teaspoon)

Extra-virgin olive oil (2 tablespoons)

Black pepper

Vegan/Dairy-free: Omit the cheese.

Mediterranean Crunch Salad

4 TO 6 SERVINGS   TIME: 25 MINUTES

This salad is a real looker — a cornucopia of roasted chickpeas, colorful peppers, and cucumbers sitting on a bed of endive. It is topped with tangy feta and a light dressing of red wine vinegar and extra-virgin olive oil, which beautifully complement this chopped salad. Perfect for entertaining!

One 15-ounce can chickpeas, drained, rinsed well, and patted dry, or 1½ cups cooked chickpeas

3 tablespoons plus 2 teaspoons extra-virgin olive oil

Sea salt

Freshly ground black pepper

2 cups diced tomato

1½ cups diced peeled English cucumber

½ cup diced red bell pepper

½ cup diced yellow bell pepper

¼ cup diced red onion

¼ cup finely chopped fresh flat-leaf parsley

2 tablespoons finely chopped fresh mint

2 tablespoons red wine vinegar

4 Belgian endives, leaves separated

1 cup crumbled good-quality feta cheese

1. Preheat the oven to 425°F.

2. Spread the chickpeas on a rimmed baking sheet. Drizzle with the 2 teaspoons of olive oil, season with ¼ teaspoon salt and ⅛ teaspoon pepper, and toss to coat. Roast for 15 minutes, stirring once halfway through. Remove from the oven and set aside.

3. Meanwhile, in a medium bowl, combine the tomato, cucumber, bell peppers, onion, parsley, and mint. Drizzle in the remaining 3 tablespoons olive oil and the vinegar. Gently stir with a wooden spoon to combine.

4. Line a serving platter with the endive leaves. Spoon the chopped vegetable mixture on top. Sprinkle with ¾ cup of the chickpeas and the feta cheese. Season with additional salt and pepper. Serve with the remaining chickpeas on the side.

From the Market

Tomatoes (2 large)

English cucumber (1 medium)

Red bell pepper (1 small)

Yellow bell pepper (1 small)

Belgian endive (4)

Red onion (1 small)

Fresh flat-leaf parsley (1 small bunch)

Fresh mint (1 small bunch)

Feta cheese, good-quality (5 ounces)

From the Pantry

Chickpeas (one 15-ounce can or 1½ cups cooked)

Extra-virgin olive oil (3 tablespoons plus 2 teaspoons)

Sea salt

Black pepper

Red wine vinegar (2 tablespoons)

Vegan/Dairy-free: Omit the cheese.

White Winter Salad

4 SERVINGS TIME: 20 MINUTES

This delightfully different salad features whisper-thin raw cauliflower, anise-flavored fennel, crunchy pear, and salty-nutty Parmesan cheese, all tossed in a lively vinaigrette. The recipe comes by way of our friend Serge Madikians of Serevan, our favorite restaurant in Dutchess County, New York.

⅓ cup sliced almonds

¼ cup white balsamic vinegar
(or Champagne vinegar)

¼ cup walnut oil (or grapeseed oil)

1½ teaspoons Dijon mustard

Kosher salt

Ground white pepper
(or freshly ground black pepper)

4 cups shaved cauliflower
(use a mandoline or very sharp knife)

½ cup shaved fennel
(use a mandoline or very sharp knife)

½ Asian pear, peeled, cored, and cut into thin slices

⅓ cup shaved Parmesan cheese

1. Place the almonds in a small dry skillet over medium heat. Toast, shaking the pan and stirring so they don't burn, until they just begin to brown, 4 to 5 minutes. Transfer the nuts to a plate to cool.

2. In a small bowl or a jar with a tight lid, combine the vinegar, oil, mustard, ¼ teaspoon salt, and ⅛ teaspoon white pepper. Whisk or shake vigorously until emulsified.

3. In a salad bowl, combine the cauliflower and fennel. Add some of the dressing and toss gently. Add the toasted almonds, Asian pear, Parmesan cheese, and more dressing to taste and toss once more. Season with salt and pepper and serve.

Food for Thought

Cauliflower is a cruciferous vegetable, like broccoli and kale, but it offers the most concentrated source of vitamin C among that family of vegetables. Vitamin C, known for its immune-boosting properties and support of bone health, may also reduce the risk of heart disease. Cauliflower is extremely low in calories (only 27 per cup) but is high in fiber, making it an excellent choice for weight loss. Additionally, cauliflower is the second largest source (behind broccoli) of carotenoids, which are beneficial for preventing chronic diseases and various forms of cancers.

From the Market
Cauliflower (1 head)
Fennel (1 small bulb)
Asian pear (1 small)
Parmesan cheese (2 ounces)
Sliced almonds (⅓ cup)
Walnut oil or grapeseed oil (¼ cup)

From the Pantry
White balsamic vinegar or Champagne vinegar (¼ cup)
Dijon mustard (1½ teaspoons)
Kosher salt
Ground white pepper or black pepper

Vegan/Dairy-free: Omit the cheese.

Vegan Taco Salad Bowl

4 SERVINGS   TIME: 50 MINUTES

We have taken an old standby, the Tex-Mex salad bowl, and turned it on its head. The homemade seitan chorizo is protein-packed and has a rich, meaty texture. This bowl is chock-full of colorful vegetables and black beans, and is tossed with a zesty lime vinaigrette. In lieu of fried tortilla chips, we top ours with crispy baked strips and drizzle it with creamy vegan sour cream. This salad may take a little more time to prepare, but in the end you have an all-in-one vegan dinner.

FOR THE SEITAN CHORIZO

½ cup vital wheat gluten flour

2 tablespoons nutritional yeast

2 teaspoons chili powder

Sea salt

1 teaspoon ground cumin

½ teaspoon paprika

½ teaspoon garlic powder

½ teaspoon onion powder

¼ teaspoon cayenne pepper

2 tablespoons ketchup

2 tablespoons organic canola oil

1 tablespoon apple cider vinegar

½ teaspoon Sriracha sauce

FOR THE TORTILLA STRIPS

Organic olive oil cooking spray

6 corn tortillas, cut in half and then sliced into ¼-inch-wide strips

Sea salt

FOR THE DRESSING

½ cup extra-virgin olive oil

2 tablespoons red wine vinegar

2 tablespoons fresh lime juice

1 teaspoon minced shallot

1 teaspoon Dijon mustard

1 teaspoon finely chopped fresh flat-leaf parsley

¾ teaspoon agave nectar

Sea salt

Freshly ground black pepper

FOR THE SALAD

3 romaine lettuce hearts, torn into bite-size pieces

¾ cup canned black beans, drained, rinsed, and patted dry, or ¾ cup cooked black beans

12 French breakfast radishes or round red radishes, trimmed and thinly sliced lengthwise

¾ cup jicama matchsticks

¾ cup frozen corn kernels, thawed, or kernels from cooked fresh corn

1 ripe avocado, sliced

12 to 14 cherry tomatoes, cut in half lengthwise

¼ cup vegan sour cream, for serving

1. Preheat the oven to 375°F.

FOR THE SEITAN CHORIZO:

2. In a large bowl, stir together the wheat gluten flour, nutritional yeast, chili powder, 1 teaspoon salt, the cumin, paprika, garlic powder, onion powder, and cayenne. Add 3 tablespoons of water, the ketchup, 1 tablespoon of the canola oil, the vinegar, and Sriracha and stir with a fork. Once incorporated, use your fingers to form the mixture into small crumbles.

3. In a large nonstick skillet over medium-high heat, heat the remaining 1 tablespoon canola oil

Continued

until shimmering. Add the seitan crumbles to the skillet. Cook undisturbed for about 30 seconds, then stir continuously with a wooden spoon, breaking it up into smaller crumbles, until nicely browned, 6 to 8 minutes. Remove from the heat and set aside.

FOR THE TORTILLA STRIPS:

4. Spray a rimmed baking sheet with the cooking spray. Place the tortilla strips on the sheet. Spray the strips with cooking spray and season with salt. Bake until crispy, 8 to 10 minutes. Set aside.

FOR THE DRESSING:

5. In a glass jar with a lid or a small bowl, combine all the dressing ingredients. Shake vigorously or whisk to emulsify.

FOR THE SALAD:

6. Place the lettuce in a large bowl, pour over half the dressing, and toss to coat. Add more dressing to taste and toss again. Arrange the dressed lettuce in four individual bowls. Place a portion of the seitan crumbles in the middle of each salad. Place a portion of the beans on one side and arrange the radishes, jicama, corn, avocado slices, and tomatoes around the top. Serve with the sour cream on the side.

From the Market
Romaine lettuce hearts (3)
French breakfast radishes or round red radishes (12)
Jicama (1 small)
Avocado, ripe (1 small)
Cherry tomatoes (12 to 14)
Shallot (1 small)
Fresh flat-leaf parsley (1 small bunch)
Lime (1)
Vegan sour cream (¼ cup)
Corn (¾ cup frozen or 1 ear)

Vital wheat gluten flour (½ cup)
Corn tortillas (6)

From the Pantry
Nutritional yeast (2 tablespoons)
Chili powder (2 teaspoons)
Sea salt
Ground cumin (1 teaspoon)
Paprika (½ teaspoon)
Garlic powder (½ teaspoon)
Onion powder (½ teaspoon)
Cayenne pepper (¼ teaspoon)
Ketchup (2 tablespoons)
Organic canola oil (2 tablespoons)

Apple cider vinegar (1 tablespoon)
Sriracha sauce (½ teaspoon)
Organic olive oil cooking spray
Extra-virgin olive oil (½ cup)
Red wine vinegar (2 tablespoons)
Dijon mustard (1 teaspoon)
Agave nectar (¾ teaspoon)
Black pepper
Black beans (one 15-ounce can or ¾ cup cooked)

New York Chopped Salad

4 TO 6 SERVINGS TIME: 45 MINUTES

Something about a big chopped salad filled with all sorts of diverse flavors and textures is supremely satisfying. Here we use carrots, celery, and radish, but the vegetables are easy to swap out for whatever you happen to have in your refrigerator. The bacon adds a salty crunch and is a natural partner for the creamy old-school Thousand Island dressing.

FOR THE SALAD

One 1-pound bone-in, skin-on chicken breast

1 tablespoon extra-virgin olive oil

Kosher salt

Freshly ground black pepper

6 slices organic uncured bacon

1 cup canned chickpeas, drained and rinsed, or 1 cup cooked chickpeas

8 cups shredded romaine lettuce hearts

1 cup diced Gruyère cheese

1 cup diced carrots

1 cup diced celery

½ cup diced red radish

½ cup diced roasted red peppers

FOR THE DRESSING

⅓ cup chili sauce

¼ cup mayonnaise

2 tablespoons diced red bell pepper

2 tablespoons sweet pickle relish

1 tablespoon finely chopped shallot

1 small clove garlic, minced

1 teaspoon Champagne vinegar, tarragon vinegar, or white wine vinegar

½ teaspoon grated fresh ginger

Kosher salt

Freshly ground black pepper

FOR THE SALAD:

1. Preheat the oven to 350°F.

2. Rub the chicken breast with the olive oil and season liberally with salt and pepper. Place the chicken on a rimmed baking sheet and bake for 30 to 35 minutes, until the temperature registers 165°F on an instant-read thermometer. Let the chicken cool slightly. Discard the skin and bones and cut the meat into ½-inch dice.

3. Meanwhile, lay the bacon slices flat on another rimmed baking sheet. Place it in the oven on a rack below the chicken and bake for 7 to 10 minutes, until starting to crisp. Remove the pan from the oven and flip the bacon. Cook for an additional 7 to 10 minutes, until crispy. Drain the bacon on a paper towel. When cool, crumble the bacon into bits. Set aside.

FOR THE DRESSING:

4. In a blender, combine all the dressing ingredients. Add ⅛ teaspoon salt and ⅛ teaspoon pepper. Puree until blended. Transfer 1 tablespoon of the dressing to a small bowl, add the chickpeas, and stir. Spoon the remaining dressing into a bowl and refrigerate, along with the bowl of chickpeas, until ready to dress the salad.

5. In a large salad bowl, combine all the salad ingredients. Spoon the dressing on the salad, toss until well coated, and serve.

From the Market

Chicken breast, bone-in, skin-on (one 1-pound breast)

Organic uncured bacon (6 slices)

Romaine lettuce hearts (24 ounces)

Carrots (3 medium)

Celery (3 stalks)

Radishes (3 medium)

Red bell pepper (1 small)

Shallot (1 small)

Garlic (1 clove)

Fresh ginger (1 small knob)

Gruyère cheese (6 ounces)

Roasted red peppers (4 ounces)

Sweet pickle relish (2 tablespoons)

Chili sauce (⅓ cup)

From the Pantry

Mayonnaise (¼ cup)

Chickpeas (one 15-ounce can or 1 cup cooked)

Champagne vinegar, tarragon vinegar, or white wine vinegar (1 teaspoon)

Extra-virgin olive oil (1 tablespoon)

Kosher salt

Black pepper

Bulgogi Beef Salad

4 SERVINGS   TIME: 45 MINUTES PLUS 30 MINUTES FREEZING

Korean-style marinated beef pairs so beautifully with all the crunchy vegetables in this elegant main course salad. The combination of the tender slices of meat and the sweet and salty dressing is irresistible. If you're not a meat-eater, you could also top this salad with a piece of grilled salmon or some tofu, or simply enjoy it on its own.

1⅓ pounds beef tenderloin or sirloin

2 teaspoons granulated sugar

FOR THE MARINADE

2 cloves garlic, minced

1 teaspoon granulated sugar

2 tablespoons low-sodium soy sauce

2 tablespoons toasted sesame oil

Freshly ground black pepper

FOR THE DRESSING

¼ cup grapeseed oil

2 tablespoons rice vinegar

1 tablespoon fresh lemon juice

1 teaspoon low-sodium soy sauce

1 tablespoon toasted sesame oil

½ teaspoon pure maple syrup

½ teaspoon chopped fresh mint

FOR THE SALAD

1 tablespoon extra-virgin olive oil

2 romaine lettuce hearts, torn into bite-size pieces

2 small heads Bibb lettuce, torn into bite-size pieces

2 carrots, sliced into rounds

2 radishes, sliced into rounds

2 Persian cucumbers, sliced in half lengthwise, seeded, and cut into half-moons

¼ cup sliced red onion, halved lengthwise and thinly cut into half-moons

½ cup cooked shelled organic edamame beans

1 Fresno chile pepper, seeded and thinly sliced

½ teaspoon chopped fresh mint

1. Place the beef in the freezer for at least 30 minutes or up to 1 hour to make it easier to slice.

2. Remove the beef from the freezer and place it on a cutting board. Using a sharp knife, slice it as thinly as possible. Put the slices of beef in a large casserole dish in two layers, sprinkling 1 teaspoon of the sugar over each layer.

FOR THE MARINADE:

3. In a small bowl, mix the garlic and sugar to make a paste. Add the soy sauce, sesame oil, and ⅛ teaspoon pepper and stir. Pour the marinade over the beef, making sure all pieces are coated (hands work well for this).

FOR THE DRESSING:

4. In a glass jar with a lid or a small bowl, combine the grapeseed oil, vinegar, lemon juice, soy sauce, sesame oil, maple syrup, and mint and shake vigorously or whisk to emulsify. Set aside.

FOR THE SALAD:

5. Heat a large grill pan over medium heat. Add the olive oil and heat until shimmering. Raise the heat to medium-high, add the beef in a single layer, and cook until nicely browned, 20 to 30 seconds per side. Transfer the cooked beef to a platter and continue cooking in batches until all the meat is cooked. Set aside.

6. Place the romaine and Bibb lettuces in a large bowl, pour over half the dressing, and toss to coat. Add additional dressing to taste and toss again. Arrange the lettuce on four individual plates. Top each salad with the carrots, radishes, cucumbers, red onion, edamame, and sliced chile. Place the beef slices on top of each salad, sprinkle with the mint, and serve.

From the Market
Beef tenderloin or sirloin (1⅓ pounds)
Romaine lettuce hearts (2)
Bibb lettuce (2 small heads)
Carrots (2 medium)
Radishes (2)
Persian cucumbers (2)
Fresno chile pepper (1)
Garlic (2 cloves)
Red onion (1 small)

Fresh mint (1 small bunch)
Lemon (1)
Organic edamame beans
(3 ounces frozen shelled)

From the Pantry
Granulated sugar (1 tablespoon)
Extra-virgin olive oil (1 tablespoon)
Low-sodium soy sauce (2 tablespoons plus 1 teaspoon)
Toasted sesame oil (3 tablespoons)

Black pepper
Grapeseed oil (¼ cup)
Rice vinegar (2 tablespoons)
Pure maple syrup (½ teaspoon)

Gluten-free: use tamari in place of soy sauce.

CHAPTER 4

Soups and Chilis

Vegan Ramen Soup with Tofu

So many ramen recipes use chicken broth and pork to build flavor. In our vegan version, we use vegetable broth along with mushrooms, miso paste, and soy sauce, which gives this soup that savory umami flavor you crave in a bowl of Asian noodles. We add tons of vegetables and bite-size pieces of tofu along with those yummy ramen noodles to make this soup flavorful and satisfying.

One 12- to 14-ounce package extra-firm organic tofu, drained, patted dry, and cut into 1-inch cubes

1 package ramen noodles (about 10 ounces)

2 tablespoons white miso paste

3 tablespoons low-sodium soy sauce or tamari

1 tablespoon extra-virgin olive oil

2 teaspoons toasted sesame oil

1 small yellow onion, coarsely chopped

2 ounces shiitake mushrooms, stemmed and sliced into ¼-inch-thick strips

2 large cloves garlic, minced

1 teaspoon finely grated fresh ginger

6 cups low-sodium vegetable broth

3 carrots, cut into slices on the diagonal

1 bunch scallions, thinly sliced, green and white parts separated

Freshly ground black pepper

½ pound baby bok choy, trimmed and leaves separated (if not available, use regular bok choy, cut into 3-inch pieces)

3 ounces baby spinach

Sriracha or hot chile sauce (optional)

1. Set a rack in the middle of the oven and preheat the oven to 350°F. Line a rimmed baking sheet with parchment paper.

2. Arrange the tofu in a single layer on the baking sheet and bake for 20 minutes, flipping once halfway through. Remove from the oven and set aside.

3. Meanwhile, bring a large pot of water to a boil. Cook the noodles according to the directions on the package. Drain and rinse under cold water. Set aside.

4. In a small bowl, whisk together the miso paste and soy sauce (or tamari) and set aside.

5. In a large stockpot over medium heat, heat the olive and sesame oils until shimmering. Add the onion and cook for 5 minutes. Add the shiitake mushrooms, garlic, and ginger and cook, stirring, for 3 minutes. Add 1 cup of the broth and, with a wooden spoon, scrape the bottom of the pan to incorporate the browned bits. Add the carrots and the scallion whites and cook for 3 minutes. Stir in the remaining 5 cups of broth and 2 cups of water. Add the miso–soy sauce mixture and ¼ teaspoon pepper and mix well.

6. Raise the heat to bring the soup to a boil, then reduce the heat to medium-low, stir in the bok choy, spinach, and tofu, and simmer for 15 minutes.

7. Divide the noodles among four to six individual serving bowls, top with the soup, tofu, and vegetables, and garnish with the scallion greens. Serve with Sriracha (or hot chile sauce) on the side, if desired.

From the Market

Ramen noodles
(1 package or about 10 ounces)

Baby spinach (3 ounces)

Baby bok choy (½ pound) or if not available, use regular bok choy

Carrots (3 medium)

Shiitake mushrooms
(2 ounces or about 5 medium)

Fresh ginger (1 knob)

Scallions (1 bunch)

Yellow onion (1 small)

Garlic (2 large cloves)

Extra-firm organic tofu
(one 12 to 14 ounce package)

From the Pantry

White miso paste
(2 tablespoons)

Low-sodium soy sauce or tamari
(3 tablespoons)

Extra-virgin olive oil (1 tablespoon)

Toasted sesame oil (2 teaspoons)

Low-sodium vegetable broth
(1½ quarts)

Black pepper

Sriracha or hot chile sauce
(optional)

*You will need parchment paper.

Roasted Cauliflower Soup with Toasted Pepitas

4 TO 6 SERVINGS TIME: 1 HOUR 10 MINUTES

The simplicity of this comforting soup belies its complex blend of flavors and textures. We roast the garlic and the cauliflower to intensify their impact, and we add a touch of cream to round out the rich broth. A topping of toasted pepitas (pumpkin seeds) adds a bit of crunch to the mix.

1 small head garlic

3 tablespoons plus 2 teaspoons extra-virgin olive oil

1 large head cauliflower, cut into 1- to 2-inch florets

Kosher salt

Freshly ground black pepper

1 tablespoon unsalted butter

1 cup chopped yellow onion

1 cup chopped carrots

2 celery stalks, chopped

4 cups low-sodium vegetable broth

3 sprigs fresh thyme

1 bay leaf

2 tablespoons raw shelled pumpkin seeds (pepitas)

2 tablespoons heavy cream (optional)

2 teaspoons white wine vinegar

1. Preheat the oven to 425°F.

2. To roast the garlic, peel away the papery outer layers, keeping the individual skins intact and the cloves attached. Trim ¼ to ½ inch off the top of the head to expose the tops of each clove. Drizzle 1½ teaspoons of the olive oil onto the exposed cloves. Wrap the head of garlic in aluminum foil and place on a rack in the oven. Roast for 30 to 35 minutes, until the garlic is soft and tender when pressed. Remove from the oven and let cool slightly.

3. Meanwhile, in a large bowl, combine the cauliflower, 2 tablespoons of the olive oil, ¼ teaspoon salt, and ⅛ teaspoon pepper. Mix well until the cauliflower is evenly coated with the oil. Spread the cauliflower on a rimmed baking sheet. Roast, with the garlic, for 25 to 30 minutes, until tender and beginning to brown, flipping halfway through the cooking time.

4. Meanwhile, begin preparing the soup. In a large stockpot over medium heat, melt the butter. Add 1 tablespoon of the olive oil. Add the onion, carrots, and celery and sauté until they soften and the onion is translucent, 7 to 8 minutes. Add the broth, 2 cups water, the thyme sprigs, and the bay leaf. Add the roasted cauliflower to the pot.

5. Squeeze the roasted garlic cloves out of their skins and into the soup and stir. Increase the heat to high and bring the soup to a boil, then reduce the heat to low and simmer, uncovered, for 20 minutes.

Continued

6. Meanwhile, in a small skillet, heat the remaining ½ teaspoon olive oil over medium heat. Add the pumpkin seeds and season with salt and pepper. Toast the seeds, shaking the pan occasionally, until they begin to brown, 3 to 5 minutes. Transfer to a plate and set aside to cool.

7. Remove the stockpot from the heat and allow the soup to cool until no longer steaming. Discard the thyme sprigs and bay leaf. Working in batches, carefully ladle the soup into a blender (place a towel on the top when blending to avoid hot splashes) or food processor and blend on high until smooth. Pour the soup into a clean pot. (As an alternative, use an immersion blender to blend the soup right in the pot.)

8. Return the soup to the heat and stir in the heavy cream, if using. Add the vinegar and 1 to 2 teaspoons salt (as desired) and pepper to taste. Ladle the soup into four to six individual bowls, top each with about 1 teaspoon of the toasted pumpkin seeds, and serve hot.

From the Market

Cauliflower (1 large head)

Carrots (2 medium)

Celery (2 stalks)

Yellow onion (1 medium)

Garlic (1 head)

Fresh thyme (3 sprigs)

Unsalted butter
(1 tablespoon)

Heavy cream
(2 tablespoons; optional)

From the Pantry

Extra-virgin olive oil
(3 tablespoons plus 2 teaspoons)

Kosher salt

Black pepper

Low-sodium vegetable broth
(1 quart)

Bay leaf (1)

Raw shelled pumpkin seeds
(pepitas) (2 tablespoons)

White wine vinegar (2 teaspoons)

Vegan/Dairy-free: use olive oil in place of butter and omit the heavy cream.

Roasted Tomato Soup with Gruyère Chickpea "Croutons"

6 TO 8 SERVINGS   TIME: 1 HOUR 40 MINUTES

Roasting the tomatoes with garlic and thyme imparts a deep, earthy flavor. The crisp and cheesy "croutons" add the perfect finishing touch, and serving the soup with a simple green salad makes this a satisfying complete meal.

FOR THE TOMATO SOUP

Two 28-ounce cans whole peeled tomatoes, drained, liquid reserved

6 cloves garlic, peeled

6 sprigs fresh thyme

Kosher salt

Freshly ground black pepper

1 teaspoon brown sugar

1 tablespoon unsalted butter

1 tablespoon extra-virgin olive oil

4 large shallots, roughly chopped

1 tablespoon tomato paste

4 cups low-sodium vegetable broth

½ cup torn fresh basil leaves

¼ teaspoon crushed red pepper flakes, or to taste

FOR THE GRUYÈRE CHICKPEA "CROUTONS"

1 tablespoon plus 1 teaspoon extra-virgin olive oil

One 15-ounce can chickpeas, drained, rinsed, and patted dry, or 1½ cups cooked chickpeas

⅓ cup finely shredded Gruyère cheese

Sea salt

Freshly ground black pepper

FOR THE TOMATO SOUP:

1. Preheat the oven to 400°F. Line a rimmed baking sheet with parchment paper.

2. Arrange the whole tomatoes in a single layer on the baking sheet. Push the garlic cloves into the fleshiest part of some of the tomatoes and lay the thyme sprigs on top. Sprinkle ½ teaspoon salt, ⅛ teaspoon pepper, and the sugar over the tomatoes. Roast for 30 to 35 minutes, until the tomatoes are tender and slightly shrunken.

3. Meanwhile, in a large stockpot over medium heat, melt the butter with the olive oil. Add the shallot, ½ teaspoon salt, and ⅛ teaspoon pepper and sauté until translucent and light golden brown, 10 to 12 minutes. Stir in the tomato paste and cook for an additional 2 minutes.

4. Add the roasted tomatoes and garlic cloves, thyme sprigs, reserved juice from the cans of tomatoes, broth, basil, and red pepper flakes and stir. Raise the heat to high, bring to a boil, then reduce the heat to low and simmer for 30 minutes.

FOR THE GRUYÈRE CHICKPEA "CROUTONS":

5. While the soup is simmering, raise the oven temperature to 425°F.

6. Pour 1 tablespoon of the olive oil into a large baking dish. Place it in the hot oven.

7. In a small bowl, combine the chickpeas, the remaining 1 teaspoon olive oil, the Gruyère cheese, ¼ teaspoon salt, and ⅛ teaspoon pepper. Mix well until the chickpeas are thoroughly coated.

Continued

8. Carefully remove the hot baking dish from the oven and pour the chickpea mixture in. Use a wooden spoon to spread the chickpeas into a single layer. Roast for 10 minutes, then stir with the wooden spoon and roast until crispy and golden brown, 5 to 7 minutes.

9. When the soup is done, working in batches, carefully ladle the soup into a blender (place a towel on the top when blending to avoid hot splashes) or food processor and blend on high until smooth. Pour the soup into a clean pot. (As an alternative, use an immersion blender to blend the soup right in the pot.) Season with an additional 1 teaspoon salt and ⅛ teaspoon pepper, or to taste.

10. Ladle the soup into serving bowls and garnish each with a handful of the chickpea "croutons." Serve hot, passing the additional "croutons" on the side.

From the Market
Garlic (6 cloves)
Shallots (4 large)
Fresh basil (1 bunch)
Fresh thyme (6 sprigs)
Gruyère cheese (1½ ounces)
Unsalted butter (1 tablespoon)

From the Pantry
Whole peeled tomatoes (two 28-ounce cans)

Kosher salt
Black pepper
Brown sugar (1 teaspoon)
Extra-virgin olive oil (2 tablespoons plus 1 teaspoon)
Tomato paste (1 tablespoon)
Low-sodium vegetable broth (1 quart)
Crushed red pepper flakes (¼ teaspoon)

Chickpeas (one 15-ounce can or 1½ cups cooked)
Sea salt
*You will need parchment paper.

 (GF)

Vegetarian French Onion Soup Gratinée

6 SERVINGS   TIME: 1 HOUR 35 MINUTES

A richly luscious broth, caramelized onions, and melted cheese are all the elements you need for a classic onion soup. In our vegetarian version, with a nod to Julia Child, we highlight all the essentials, then top them with slices of toasted baguette and Gruyère cheese, browned and bubbling.

3 tablespoons unsalted butter

1 tablespoon extra-virgin olive oil, plus extra for drizzling

10 cups thinly sliced Spanish onion

Kosher salt

¼ teaspoon granulated sugar

3 tablespoons all-purpose flour

8 cups low-sodium vegetable broth

1 cup dry white wine

Freshly ground black pepper

3 tablespoons cognac

Six 1-inch-thick slices French baguette

1 large clove garlic, cut in half

2 cups grated Gruyère cheese

1. In a large stockpot over low heat, melt the butter. Add the olive oil and the onion. Cover and cook, stirring occasionally, for 15 minutes. Uncover, raise the heat to medium, and stir in 1 teaspoon salt and the sugar. Cook uncovered, stirring often, for 30 minutes, or until the onion is deep golden brown.

2. Sprinkle in the flour and mix for 3 minutes to incorporate. Remove the pot from the heat.

3. Preheat the oven to 325°F.

4. Meanwhile, in a separate pot, bring the broth to a boil. Stir the broth into the stockpot with the onion. Set the stockpot over low heat and bring to a simmer. Add the wine, ½ teaspoon salt, and ⅛ teaspoon pepper. Partially cover, and cook, stirring occasionally, for 20 minutes. Add the cognac and simmer for 10 minutes.

5. While the soup is simmering, place the baguette slices on a rimmed baking sheet and toast in the oven for 15 minutes. Remove from the oven, flip, and drizzle each slice with olive oil, then rub each one with the cut garlic clove. Return the slices to the oven and toast until beginning to brown, about 15 minutes. Remove from the oven and set the oven to broil.

6. Arrange six ovenproof soup bowls on a rimmed baking sheet. Sprinkle 1 tablespoon of the grated cheese on the bottom of each. Fill each bowl three-quarters full with soup. Top with the toasted baguette slices and cover the toast and the soup with about 4 tablespoons of grated cheese per bowl. Place the baking sheet under the broiler and broil until the cheese is bubbling, 2 to 3 minutes. Remove from the oven and serve hot.

From the Market
Spanish onion (3 pounds)
Garlic (1 large clove)
Unsalted butter (3 tablespoons)
Gruyère cheese (8 ounces)
Cognac (3 tablespoons)
French baguette (1)

From the Pantry
Extra-virgin olive oil (1 tablespoon, plus extra for drizzling)
Kosher salt
Granulated sugar (¼ teaspoon)
All-purpose flour (3 tablespoons)

Low-sodium vegetable broth (2 quarts)
Dry white wine (1 cup)
Black pepper

Kale, Tomato, and Cannellini Bean Soup

6 SERVINGS TIME: 1 HOUR 10 MINUTES

This is such a hearty, nourishing, and satisfying soup. What's more, it's also incredibly easy to prepare, inexpensive to make, and tastes even better the next day and the day after that. Need we say more?

2 tablespoons extra-virgin olive oil

1 medium onion, diced

4 cloves garlic, minced

2 large carrots, diced

4 celery stalks, diced

4 cups low-sodium vegetable broth

One 28-ounce can tomato puree

One 2-inch Parmesan cheese rind (optional)

3 fresh thyme sprigs

2 bay leaves

Sea salt

Freshly ground black pepper

Two 15-ounce cans cannellini beans, drained and rinsed, or 3 cups cooked

1 bunch lacinato (dinosaur or Tuscan) kale, stems and tough center ribs removed, leaves roughly chopped (about 6 cups packed)

1. In a large stockpot over medium heat, heat the olive oil until shimmering. Add the onion and cook, stirring occasionally, until slightly translucent, 5 to 7 minutes. Add the garlic and cook for another minute.

2. Add the carrots and celery and cook, stirring occasionally, for 10 minutes, or until softened. Pour in the broth and tomato puree. Add the Parmesan rind, thyme, bay leaves, 2 teaspoons salt, and ¼ teaspoon pepper, cover, and bring to a boil. Reduce the heat to maintain a simmer and cook for 20 minutes.

3. Add the cannellini beans and kale and cook, stirring occasionally, for an additional 15 minutes. Discard the Parmesan rind, thyme, and bay leaves. Season with additional salt and pepper and serve hot.

Food for Thought

White beans, such as cannellini, great northern, and navy, are a great vegetarian source of iron—24 percent of the daily recommended intake. They are also an excellent source of fiber, protein, and calcium, and contain impressive amounts of folate, potassium, and manganese. White beans are low on the glycemic index and offer major weight loss benefits.

From the Market
Lacinato (dinosaur or Tuscan) kale (1 bunch)

Carrots (2 large)

Celery (4 stalks)

Onion (1 medium)

Garlic (4 cloves)

Fresh thyme (3 sprigs)

Parmesan cheese rind (one 2-inch rind; optional)

From the Pantry
Extra-virgin olive oil (2 tablespoons)

Low-sodium vegetable broth (1 quart)

Tomato puree (one 28-ounce can)

Bay leaves (2)

Sea salt

Black pepper

Cannellini beans (two 15-ounce cans or 3 cups cooked)

Vegan/Dairy-free: omit Parmesan rind.

Udon Noodle Soup with Miso-Glazed Vegetables and Chicken

6 SERVINGS TIME: 1 HOUR

Udon noodle soup is traditionally made with a pork broth, but we were eager to make one with a rich chicken stock. We have upped the amount of vegetables in the soup to make it a vibrant, substantial dinner. Glazing the vegetables and chicken with miso before adding them to the broth gives them a deep umami flavor.

8 dried shiitake mushrooms

1 cup boiling water

FOR THE MISO-GLAZED VEGETABLES AND CHICKEN

4 tablespoons mirin

2 tablespoons low-sodium soy sauce

2 tablespoons vegetable oil

2 tablespoons white miso paste

2 teaspoons minced fresh ginger

2 teaspoons toasted sesame oil

6 to 8 baby bok choy, halved (if not available, use 2 regular bok choy, cut lengthwise into eighths)

3 cups 1-inch broccoli florets

5 to 6 sliced fresh shiitake mushrooms, ¼ inch thick

2 carrots, sliced and cut on the diagonal, ¼ inch thick

1½ pounds skinless chicken breast, cut into ¼-inch-thick strips

FOR THE SOUP

1 tablespoon vegetable oil

1 teaspoon toasted sesame oil

1 teaspoon minced fresh ginger

2 teaspoons minced garlic

1 cup sliced scallions, white and light green parts only, separated

1 tablespoon white miso paste

1 tablespoon low-sodium soy sauce

5 cups low-sodium chicken broth

Sea salt

Freshly ground black pepper

One 8-ounce package udon noodles

1 lime, cut into 6 wedges

1. Set the racks in the middle and lower thirds of the oven and preheat the oven to 400°F.

2. Place the dried shiitake mushrooms in a bowl, cover with the boiling water, and set aside to reconstitute.

FOR THE MISO-GLAZED VEGETABLES AND CHICKEN:

3. Evenly divide the mirin, soy sauce, vegetable oil, white miso paste, ginger, and sesame oil between two large bowls. Mix well. Place the bok choy, broccoli, fresh shiitakes, and carrots in one of the bowls and toss until the vegetables are well coated. Place the chicken strips in the other bowl and toss until well coated.

4. Arrange all the vegetables in a single layer on a rimmed baking sheet. Roast for 10 minutes. Remove from the oven and, using tongs or a spatula, flip the vegetables. Return the vegetables to the oven. Arrange the chicken strips in a single layer on another rimmed baking sheet and place in the oven with the vegetables. Roast the chicken and vegetables for 10 minutes. Remove both pans from the oven and set aside.

Continued

FOR THE SOUP:

5. Drain the reconstituted mushrooms, reserving the soaking liquid, and slice them. Strain the soaking liquid to remove any grit. Set both aside.

6. In a large stockpot over medium-high heat, heat the vegetable and sesame oils until shimmering. Add the sliced reconstituted mushrooms, ginger, garlic, and ¾ cup of the sliced scallions. Cook, stirring continuously, until lightly browned, about 2 minutes. Add the miso and soy sauce and cook, stirring, for an additional 2 minutes. Add the broth, the reserved mushroom soaking liquid, and 2 cups water. Bring to a boil, then reduce the heat to low. Season with 1 teaspoon salt and ¼ teaspoon pepper and simmer for 20 minutes.

7. Meanwhile, bring a large pot of water to a boil. Add the noodles and cook according to the directions on the package. Drain and set aside.

8. Strain the broth, discarding the solids.

9. Place the noodles into six individual bowls and add glazed vegetables and chicken to each, dividing them evenly. Ladle the soup into each bowl and top with the remaining scallions and the lime wedges. Serve hot.

From the Market
Udon noodles (one 8-ounce package)
Chicken breast (1½ pounds)
Baby bok choy (6 to 8) or if not available, use regular bok choy (2)
Broccoli (1 head)
Fresh shiitake mushrooms (4 ounces)
Carrots (2 medium)
Scallions (2 bunches)
Fresh ginger (1 small knob)
Garlic (1 large clove)
Lime (1)
Dried shiitake mushrooms (8)

From the Pantry
Mirin (4 tablespoons)
Low-sodium soy sauce (3 tablespoons)
Vegetable oil (3 tablespoons)
White miso paste (2 tablespoons)
Toasted sesame oil (3 teaspoons)
Low-sodium chicken broth (5 cups)
Sea salt
Black pepper

Green Split Pea and Zucchini Soup with Rutabaga

4 TO 6 SERVINGS TIME: 1 HOUR PLUS SOAKING TIME

Pulses are rich in nutrients and fiber, a terrific source of protein, and available all year long. Our split pea soup is made with zucchini and rutabaga—a root vegetable that is a cross between a cabbage and a turnip. The combination adds an unexpected sweet and savory flavor to this hearty soup.

FOR THE SOUP

1½ cups dried green split peas

2 tablespoons extra-virgin olive oil

1½ cups chopped yellow onion

2 cloves garlic, minced

¾ cup peeled and diced rutabaga cut into ½-inch cubes

2½ cups diced zucchini cut into ½-inch cubes

½ teaspoon ground turmeric

8 cups low-sodium vegetable broth

Kosher salt

Freshly ground black pepper

FOR THE CROUTONS

½ baguette, cut into ½-inch cubes (about 4 cups)

2 tablespoons extra-virgin olive oil

2 cloves garlic, minced

FOR THE SOUP:

1. Place the split peas in a bowl, cover with water, and soak for several hours or overnight at room temperature. Drain and rinse the peas in cold water.

2. In a large stockpot over medium-high heat, heat the olive oil until shimmering. Add the onion and cook until translucent, about 2 minutes. Add the garlic and rutabaga and cook, stirring, until it begins to soften, about 2 minutes. Add the zucchini and sauté for 1 minute. Add the split peas, turmeric, and broth and mix well.

3. Raise the heat to high and bring to a boil. Reduce the heat to medium-low and simmer uncovered, stirring occasionally, for 45 minutes to 1 hour, until the split peas are tender. Add 2 teaspoons salt and ¼ teaspoon pepper and stir.

4. Carefully ladle half the soup into a blender (place a towel on the top when blending to avoid hot splashes) or food processor and puree. Pour the pureed soup back into the pot with the remaining soup and simmer until hot.

FOR THE CROUTONS:

5. Preheat the oven to 350°F.

6. In a large bowl, combine the bread, olive oil, and garlic and mix together well. Spread the bread out on a rimmed baking sheet and bake until golden brown and toasted, 15 to 20 minutes, flipping with a spatula halfway through.

7. Ladle the soup into individual bowls, top with croutons, and serve.

From the Market

Green split peas (1½ cups dried)

Zucchini (2 medium)

Rutabaga (1 small)

Yellow onions (2 small)

Garlic (4 cloves)

Baguette (½)

From the Pantry

Extra-virgin olive oil (4 tablespoons)

Low-sodium vegetable broth (2 quarts)

Ground turmeric (½ teaspoon)

Kosher salt

Black pepper

Gluten-free: omit the croutons.

Caldo Verde with Kale and Chorizo

4 TO 6 SERVINGS TIME: 1 HOUR

Caldo verde stands as the Portuguese contribution to the world's great culinary traditions. In this hearty stew-like soup, slices of chorizo swim in a fragrant broth filled with kale and potatoes. The chorizo adds earthy heat, the potatoes add creaminess, and the kale lends the perfect texture.

1 pound fresh uncured (Mexican) chorizo links, cut into ¼-inch-thick rounds

2 cups chopped yellow onion

3 cloves garlic, minced

2 cups peeled and diced red or Yukon Gold potatoes, cut into ½-inch cubes

8 cups thinly sliced kale, stems and ribs removed

8 cups low-sodium chicken broth

1 tablespoon balsamic vinegar

Kosher salt

Freshly ground black pepper

1. In a large stockpot over medium heat, cook the chorizo slices in a single layer, undisturbed, until lightly browned, 2 to 3 minutes. Continue cooking, stirring, until they've rendered their fat, an additional 2 to 3 minutes. Add the onion and garlic and sauté until the onion is translucent, about 4 minutes. Stir in the potatoes and cook for an additional 2 minutes. Add half the kale and sauté until wilted, about 2 minutes, then add the remaining kale and cook for an additional 2 minutes. Add the broth, vinegar, 1 teaspoon salt, and ⅛ teaspoon pepper.

2. Bring the broth to a boil. Reduce the heat to maintain a simmer, partially cover the pot, and cook until the potatoes are fork-tender, about 30 minutes.

3. Ladle into soup bowls and serve.

From the Market

Fresh uncured (Mexican) chorizo links (1 pound)

Kale (1 pound)

Red or Yukon Gold potatoes (4 small)

Yellow onion (1 large)

Garlic (3 cloves)

From the Pantry

Low-sodium chicken broth (2 quarts)

Balsamic vinegar (1 tablespoon)

Kosher salt

Black pepper

Red Lentil and Bean Chili

6 TO 8 SERVINGS TIME: 1 HOUR

Who doesn't love a hot bowl of chili on a cold winter day? Eating a mostly plant-based diet doesn't mean you have to sacrifice this simple pleasure. In our vegetarian version of this traditional dish, beans and red lentils take center stage. The lentils add a sweet and nutty flavor that helps to balance the heat of the chili and jalapeños. It's so hearty and comforting, even meat eaters won't know what's missing!

FOR THE SEASONING MIX

3 tablespoons chili powder

2 teaspoons ground cumin

1½ teaspoons paprika

1 teaspoon dried oregano

¼ teaspoon crushed red pepper flakes, or to taste

1½ teaspoons kosher salt

⅛ teaspoon freshly ground black pepper

FOR THE CHILI

2 tablespoons grapeseed oil

2 cups chopped yellow onion

1 cup chopped red bell pepper

1 cup chopped carrots

½ cup chopped celery

4 cloves garlic, minced

1 jalapeño pepper, minced

2 tablespoons tomato paste

One 28-ounce can crushed tomatoes

2 cups low-sodium vegetable broth

1 tablespoon low-sodium soy sauce

1 bay leaf

1 cup dried red lentils, rinsed and drained

One 15-ounce can black beans, drained and rinsed, or 1½ cups cooked black beans

One 15-ounce can kidney beans, drained and rinsed, or 1½ cups cooked kidney beans

Kosher salt

Freshly ground black pepper

Cooked rice or tortillas, for serving

Toppings of your choice: avocado, pickled jalapeño peppers, sour cream, shredded Monterey Jack or cheddar cheese, vegan cheese

FOR THE SEASONING MIX:

1. Combine all the seasoning mix ingredients in a small bowl and stir. Set aside.

FOR THE CHILI:

2. In a large stockpot over medium heat, heat the grapeseed oil until shimmering. Add the onion and sauté for 1 minute. Add the bell pepper, carrots, and celery. Sauté until softened, about 10 minutes. Add the garlic and jalapeño pepper and sauté for an additional minute. Add the tomato paste and seasoning mix and stir well to incorporate. Add the crushed tomatoes, broth, soy sauce, and bay leaf and stir well.

3. Raise the heat to medium-high and bring to a boil. Stir in the lentils and reduce the heat to maintain a simmer. Cook, partially covered, stirring occasionally, until the lentils are just tender, 15 to 17 minutes.

4. Stir in the beans and simmer the chili, partially covered, for an additional 10 minutes. Discard the bay leaf. Season with salt and black pepper.

5. Ladle the chili into individual bowls. Serve hot, with rice or tortillas and the toppings of your choice.

From the Market

Red bell pepper (1 large)

Celery (2 stalks)

Carrots (2 medium)

Jalapeño pepper (1 medium)

Yellow onion (1 large)

Garlic (4 cloves)

Rice or tortillas

Toppings of your choice: avocado, pickled jalapeño peppers, sour cream, shredded Monterey Jack or cheddar cheese, vegan cheese

From the Pantry

Chili powder (3 tablespoons)

Ground cumin (2 teaspoons)

Paprika (1½ teaspoons)

Dried oregano (1 teaspoon)

Crushed red pepper flakes (¼ teaspoon)

Kosher salt

Black pepper

Grapeseed oil (2 tablespoons)

Tomato paste (2 tablespoons)

Crushed tomatoes (one 28-ounce can)

Low-sodium vegetable broth (2 cups)

Low-sodium soy sauce (1 tablespoon)

Bay leaf (1)

Red lentils (1 cup dried)

Black beans (one 15-ounce can or 1½ cups cooked)

Kidney beans (one 15-ounce can or 1½ cups cooked)

Gluten-free: use tamari in place of soy sauce.

Vegetable-Loaded Turkey Chili

The secret of any chili is in its seasoning mix, and our turkey chili gains smoky dimension and heat from the addition of chipotle peppers in adobo sauce. The combination of corn, zucchini, and sweet red pepper is unexpected in chili, but it adds a welcome sweetness and lightness to this dish.

FOR THE SEASONING MIX

2 tablespoons chili powder

1½ teaspoons paprika

1 teaspoon dried oregano

1 teaspoon ground cumin

1 teaspoon ground coriander

½ teaspoon ground cinnamon

½ teaspoon crushed red pepper flakes, or to taste

⅛ teaspoon cayenne pepper

1½ teaspoons kosher salt

⅛ teaspoon freshly ground black pepper

FOR THE CHILI

1 tablespoon extra-virgin olive oil

1 pound ground turkey

1 cup chopped yellow onion

5 cloves garlic, minced

1 tablespoon chopped chipotle peppers in adobo sauce

2 cups diced zucchini, cut into ½-inch cubes

1 cup diced red bell pepper, cut into ½-inch pieces

1 cup fresh or frozen corn kernels

One 28-ounce can crushed tomatoes

One 15-ounce can black beans, drained and rinsed, or 1½ cups cooked black beans

Kosher salt

Freshly ground black pepper

Cooked rice or tortillas, for serving

Toppings of your choice: pickled jalapeño peppers, grated cheese, sour cream, avocado, red onion

FOR THE SEASONING MIX:

1. Combine all the seasoning mix ingredients in a small bowl and stir well. Set aside.

FOR THE CHILI:

2. In a large Dutch oven over medium-high heat, heat the olive oil until shimmering. Add the ground turkey and cook, breaking it up with a wooden spoon, until no longer pink, about 4 minutes. Stir in the onion and garlic and cook until translucent, about 2 minutes. Add the seasoning mix and the chipotle pepper and cook, stirring to thoroughly blend with the onion mixture, for an additional 2 minutes. Add the zucchini, bell pepper, and corn and cook, stirring, until the vegetables are softened, about 4 minutes. Pour in the crushed tomatoes and 1 cup water. Bring to a boil. Reduce the heat to low, add the black beans, partially cover, and simmer, stirring occasionally, until thick, about 30 minutes. (If the chili is too thick, add additional water to reach the desired consistency.) Season with salt and black pepper.

3. Ladle the chili into four to six individual serving bowls. Serve hot, with the toppings of your choice.

SINCE SO LITTLE OF THE CANNED CHIPOTLE PEPPER IN ADOBO SAUCE IS USED IN THIS RECIPE, TRANSFER WHAT IS LEFT IN THE CAN TO A GLASS JAR AND STORE IN THE REFRIGERATOR, WHERE IT WILL KEEP FOR WEEKS. THESE PEPPERS AND SAUCE ARE TERRIFIC INGREDIENTS TO ADD DEPTH AND HEAT TO ANY DISH, SUCH AS EGGS, TACOS, AND GRAIN BOWLS.

From the Market

Ground turkey (1 pound)

Red bell pepper (1 small)

Zucchini (2 small)

Corn (2 medium ears fresh or
1 cup frozen)

Yellow onion (1 medium)

Garlic (5 cloves)

Chipotle peppers in adobo sauce
(one 7-ounce can)

Rice or tortillas

Toppings of your choice: pickled
jalapeño peppers, grated cheese,
sour cream, avocado, red onion

From the Pantry

Chili powder (2 tablespoons)

Paprika (1½ teaspoons)

Dried oregano (1 teaspoon)

Ground cumin (1 teaspoon)

Ground coriander (1 teaspoon)

Ground cinnamon (½ teaspoon)

Crushed red pepper flakes
(½ teaspoon)

Cayenne pepper (½ teaspoon)

Kosher salt

Black pepper

Extra-virgin olive oil
(1 tablespoon)

Crushed tomatoes
(one 28-ounce can)

Black beans (one 15-ounce can
or 1½ cups cooked)

CHAPTER 5

Burgers, Patties, and Sandwiches

Spinach, Mushroom, and Feta Cutlets

4 TO 5 SERVINGS   TIME: 40 MINUTES

This is one of our favorite go-to vegetarian recipes. Inspired by our love for the Greek dish spanakopita, these cutlets are filled with spinach and tangy feta cheese along with lots of mushrooms, giving them a meaty, umami dimension. We like to top these savory cutlets with mango chutney—you can make your own, but if you don't have time, there are some surprisingly good options available at grocery stores.

3 large eggs

Kosher salt

Freshly ground black pepper

3 cups finely chopped white button mushrooms, stems trimmed

4 scallions, white and light green parts only, finely chopped

One 10-ounce package frozen chopped spinach, thawed and squeezed to remove excess liquid

⅔ cup plain bread crumbs

¾ cup finely crumbled good-quality feta cheese

3 tablespoons extra-virgin olive oil

1¼ cups Mango Chutney (page 226) or your favorite store-bought chutney

1. Preheat the oven to 300°F.

2. In a large bowl, beat together the eggs, ½ teaspoon salt, and ⅛ teaspoon pepper. Using a wooden spoon, stir in the mushrooms and scallions. Add the spinach and mix well. Gently fold in the bread crumbs and feta cheese and stir until blended.

3. Shape a handful of the mixture into a patty about 3 inches wide and ½ inch thick. Place the formed patty on a baking sheet or platter and repeat with the remaining mixture. (You should have 8 to 10 patties.)

4. In a large nonstick skillet over medium-high heat, heat 1½ tablespoons of the olive oil until shimmering. Carefully place half of the patties in the pan and cook undisturbed until golden brown, 3 to 4 minutes. Flip the patties and cook until the second side is golden brown, an additional 3 to 4 minutes. Transfer the patties to a rimmed baking sheet and place in the oven to keep warm. Wipe the skillet clean with paper towel, add the remaining 1½ tablespoons olive oil, and cook the remaining patties.

5. Transfer all the patties to a platter and serve with the mango chutney on the side.

From the Market

White button mushrooms (20 to 24, about ¾ pound)

Scallions (4)

Frozen chopped spinach (one 10-ounce package)

Large eggs (3)

Feta cheese, good-quality (4 ounces)

Mango Chutney (1¼ cups; page 226, or your favorite store-bought)

From the Pantry

Kosher salt

Black pepper

Plain bread crumbs (⅔ cup)

Extra-virgin olive oil (3 tablespoons)

White Bean and Kale Quesadillas with Roasted Tomatillo Salsa

4 SERVINGS TIME: 40 MINUTES

This combination hits all the right marks: creamy white beans, gooey cheese, and earthy kale, finished with a fabulously flavorful salsa verde. Serve with a salad, soup, or sliced avocado for a simple, savory, and healthy meal.

2 tablespoons extra-virgin olive oil

3 tablespoons minced shallot

1 clove garlic, minced

Two 15-ounce cans cannellini beans, drained and rinsed, or 3 cups cooked cannellini beans

1 tablespoon finely chopped fresh flat-leaf parsley

Kosher salt

Freshly ground black pepper

5 cups roughly chopped lacinato (dinosaur or Tuscan) kale, stems removed

2 to 3 tablespoons unsalted butter

Ten 8- to 10-inch multigrain or whole wheat flour tortillas

2½ cups shredded Monterey Jack cheese

¾ cup Roasted Tomatillo Salsa (page 230) or your favorite store-bought salsa

1. Preheat the oven to 250°F.

2. In a medium nonstick skillet over medium heat, heat 1 tablespoon of the olive oil until shimmering. Add the shallot and cook until translucent, 2 to 3 minutes. Add the garlic and cook for an additional minute. Add the beans, parsley, ¼ teaspoon salt, and ⅛ teaspoon pepper and mix well. Cook until the beans are hot, about 3 minutes. Transfer to a bowl and mash the beans with a fork, leaving a few chunks for texture.

3. Wipe out the skillet, return it to medium heat, and add the remaining 1 tablespoon olive oil. Once the oil is shimmering, add the kale and sauté until wilted, about 4 minutes. Season with salt and pepper. Set aside.

4. In a grill pan or a separate large skillet over medium heat, melt a small pat of the butter. Place a tortilla in the pan and sprinkle 3 tablespoons of the cheese over the entire tortilla. Cook until the cheese has melted, then distribute about 2 tablespoons of the white bean mixture and some of the kale over just *half* the tortilla. With a spatula, fold the tortilla in half to sandwich the filling. Sprinkle the folded tortilla with a pinch of salt. Cook until the bottom is golden brown, about 1 minute, then flip, sprinkle with an additional pinch of salt, and cook until golden brown on the second side, about 1 minute more. Transfer to a rimmed baking sheet and place in the oven to keep warm. Repeat with the remaining tortillas, cheese, filling, and kale.

5. Remove the quesadillas from the oven, cut each in half, and serve with the salsa.

From the Market

Lacinato (dinosaur or Tuscan) kale
(1 bunch)

Fresh flat-leaf parsley (1 small bunch)

Shallot (1 large)

Garlic (1 clove)

Unsalted butter (2 to 3 tablespoons)

Monterey Jack cheese (10 ounces)

Multigrain or whole wheat flour
tortillas (ten 8- to 10-inch tortillas)

Roasted Tomatillo Salsa (¾ cup;
page 230, or your favorite store-
bought)

From the Pantry

Extra-virgin olive oil
(2 tablespoons)

Cannellini beans
(two 15-ounce cans or
3 cups cooked)

Kosher salt

Black pepper

Chicken and Vegetable Burgers
with the Works

4 SERVINGS TIME: 45 MINUTES

Ground chicken is a great alternative to turkey or beef when looking for another burger option. We do half dark meat and half white meat to keep these burgers juicy. Incorporating zucchini not only adds more moisture but also adds a wonderful flavor. This burger is great on a bun with the works but is also terrific on top of a big salad for a lighter dinner.

1 pound ground chicken, preferably half dark and half white meat

¾ cup coarsely grated zucchini, excess liquid squeezed out

2 tablespoons grated yellow onion, drained of liquid

2 tablespoons ketchup

1 tablespoon Worcestershire sauce

1 large clove garlic, minced

1 tablespoon chopped fresh basil

1 tablespoon chopped fresh flat-leaf parsley

1 tablespoon thinly sliced scallion, white and light green parts only

Kosher salt

Freshly ground black pepper

1 tablespoon vegetable oil (or organic canola oil), plus extra for coating hands

4 hamburger buns, preferably whole wheat or multigrain

Toppings of your choice: sliced tomato, sliced avocado, sliced red onion or Pickled Red Onions (page 225), lettuce, mayonnaise

1. Place the chicken in a large bowl. Add the zucchini, onion, ketchup, Worcestershire, garlic, basil, parsley, scallion, 1 teaspoon salt, and ½ teaspoon pepper and mix well.

2. Lightly coat your hands with vegetable oil and form the chicken mixture into 4 patties (they will be quite moist). Place on a platter or rimmed baking sheet and refrigerate for 15 minutes to firm up.

3. In a nonstick griddle or large nonstick skillet over medium-high heat, heat the vegetable oil. Arrange the patties in the pan and cook until browned, 4 to 5 minutes. Flip the burgers and cook for an additional 4 to 5 minutes, until cooked through.

4. Place the burgers on the buns and serve with your favorite toppings.

From the Market

Ground chicken (1 pound, preferably half dark and half white meat)

Zucchini (2 small or 1 medium)

Yellow onion (1 small)

Garlic (1 clove)

Fresh basil (1 small bunch)

Fresh flat-leaf parsley (1 small bunch)

Scallion (1)

Hamburger buns, preferably whole wheat or multigrain (4)

Toppings of your choice: tomato, avocado, red onion or Pickled Red Onions (page 225), lettuce, mayonnaise

From the Pantry

Ketchup (2 tablespoons)

Worcestershire sauce (1 tablespoon)

Kosher salt

Black pepper

Vegetable or organic canola oil (1 tablespoon plus extra for coating hands)

Gluten-free: use gluten-free buns.

Transcendent Burgers

6 SERVINGS   TIME: 1 HOUR 30 MINUTES

These robust veggie burgers are both flavor-packed and intensely satisfying. The mushrooms deliver that delicious umami flavor while the quinoa and black beans add the desired crispness and double the amount of protein. We love that these burgers are super moist without being mushy. Serve on a warm toasted bun with your favorite toppings and a dash of Zen, and you will be transported to a state of bliss.

3 cups 1-inch cauliflower florets

5 tablespoons extra-virgin olive oil

1 medium yellow onion, chopped

2 cloves garlic, minced

Kosher salt

Freshly ground black pepper

One 15-ounce can black beans, drained and rinsed, or 1 ½ cups cooked black beans

¾ cup cooked quinoa

½ cup panko bread crumbs

1 tablespoon ketchup

1 tablespoon nutritional yeast

6 cremini mushrooms, stems trimmed, cut into quarters

½ teaspoon paprika

6 hamburger buns, preferably whole wheat or multigrain

Toppings of your choice: sliced tomato, sliced avocado, sliced red onion, lettuce, pickles

1. Place the cauliflower florets in a food processor. Pulse until broken down into tiny pieces resembling couscous. Set aside.

2. In a large skillet over medium heat, heat 1 tablespoon of the olive oil until shimmering. Add the onion and cook, stirring, for 8 to 10 minutes, until soft and slightly browned. Add the cauliflower, garlic, 1 teaspoon salt, and ¼ teaspoon pepper. Raise the heat to medium-high and cook for 3 minutes. Remove from the heat.

3. Line a baking sheet with parchment paper.

4. In a food processor, combine the cauliflower mixture, black beans, quinoa, bread crumbs, ketchup, nutritional yeast, mushrooms, paprika, ½ teaspoon salt, and ¼ teaspoon pepper. Pulse until combined. Using a spatula or wooden spoon, scrape down the sides of the processor bowl. Pulse again until combined but not mushy.

5. Form the mixture into 6 patties and set them on the prepared baking sheet. Refrigerate for 15 to 30 minutes.

6. In a large nonstick pan over medium heat, heat 2 tablespoons of the olive oil until shimmering. Add half the patties and cook undisturbed until browned, 4 to 5 minutes. Flip and cook until browned, an additional 4 to 5 minutes. Transfer the burgers to a plate. Heat the remaining 2 tablespoons olive oil and repeat with the remaining patties.

7. Place the burgers on the buns and serve with your favorite toppings.

From the Market

Cauliflower (1 head)

Cremini (baby bella) mushrooms (6 medium)

Yellow onion (1 medium)

Garlic (2 cloves)

Hamburger buns, preferably whole wheat or multigrain (6)

Toppings of your choice: tomato, avocado, red onion, lettuce, pickles

From the Pantry

Extra-virgin olive oil (¼ cup plus 1 tablespoon)

Kosher salt

Black pepper

Black beans (one 15-ounce can or 1 ½ cups cooked)

Quinoa (¼ cup dried)

Panko bread crumbs (½ cup)

Ketchup (1 tablespoon)

Nutritional yeast (1 tablespoon)

Paprika (½ teaspoon)

*You will need parchment paper.

Savory Tuna Burgers with Sriracha Mayonnaise

4 SERVINGS   TIME: 40 MINUTES

The vibrant mix of spices makes this burger one you'll return to again and again. It's bright with ginger, cilantro, and garlic and stays juicy and tender whether grilled outdoors or on a grill pan on the stove. We like serving it with a spicy-creamy sauce made from Sriracha, mayonnaise, ginger, and soy sauce.

1½ pounds sushi-quality raw tuna

FOR THE SRIRACHA MAYONNAISE

¾ cup mayonnaise

1 tablespoon Sriracha sauce, or to taste

1 tablespoon low-sodium soy sauce

1 teaspoon finely grated fresh ginger

FOR THE TUNA BURGERS

3 tablespoons Dijon mustard

2 tablespoons low-sodium soy sauce

2 tablespoons chopped fresh cilantro

1½ tablespoons grated yellow onion

1 tablespoon toasted sesame oil

1 tablespoon minced garlic

2 teaspoons rice vinegar

½ teaspoon finely grated fresh ginger

¼ teaspoon cayenne pepper

Kosher salt

Freshly ground black pepper

1 tablespoon extra-virgin olive oil, or more as needed, for brushing the patties

Organic olive oil cooking spray

4 hamburger buns, preferably whole wheat or multigrain

Toppings of your choice: sliced tomato, sliced avocado, sliced red onion, lettuce, pickles

1. Place the tuna in the freezer for 10 to 15 minutes, until firm to the touch (this makes it easier to slice).

FOR THE SRIRACHA MAYONNAISE:

2. Meanwhile, in a small bowl, stir together all the Sriracha mayonnaise ingredients until thoroughly combined. Set aside.

FOR THE TUNA BURGERS:

3. Remove the tuna from the freezer and place it on a cutting board. Using a large, sharp knife, chop the tuna to the size and texture of hamburger meat.

4. In a medium bowl, combine the mustard, soy sauce, cilantro, onion, sesame oil, garlic, vinegar, ginger, cayenne pepper, ½ teaspoon salt, and ⅛ teaspoon black pepper. Add the tuna and mix thoroughly to combine. Divide the mixture into 4 equal patties about 3½ inches wide and 1 inch thick and lightly brush them on both sides with olive oil. Place the patties on a plate or platter and refrigerate for 10 to 15 minutes.

5. Heat a grill pan over medium-high heat. Spray the pan with cooking spray and add the burgers. Cook for 2 minutes on each side for rare, 3 to 4 minutes for medium-rare. Place the burgers on the buns, spread them lightly with the Sriracha mayonnaise, and serve with your favorite toppings.

From the Market

Fresh tuna, sushi-quality
(1½ pounds)

Fresh ginger (1 small knob)

Yellow onion (1 small)

Garlic (3 cloves)

Fresh cilantro (1 small bunch)

Hamburger buns, preferably
whole wheat or multigrain (4)

Toppings of your choice:
tomato, avocado, red onion,
lettuce, pickles

From the Pantry

Mayonnaise (¾ cup)

Sriracha sauce (1 tablespoon)

Low-sodium soy sauce
(3 tablespoons)

Dijon mustard (3 tablespoons)

Toasted sesame oil (1 tablespoon)

Rice vinegar (2 teaspoons)

Cayenne pepper (¼ teaspoon)

Kosher salt

Black pepper

Extra-virgin olive oil
(1 tablespoon, or more as needed)

Organic olive oil cooking spray

Gluten-free: use tamari in place of
soy sauce and use gluten-free buns.

Cauliflower, Spinach, and Chickpea Patties

6 SERVINGS   TIME: 1 HOUR 15 MINUTES

These chickpea patties are packed with the added goodness of cauliflower, spinach, red pepper, and scallions, giving them a wonderful light flavor and texture. Then we add tasty Mediterranean herbs and spices, such as cumin, turmeric, and parsley. The end result? A great-tasting dish, chock-full of legume protein and nutritious vegetables.

3 cups 2-inch cauliflower florets

One 15-ounce can chickpeas, drained and rinsed, or 1½ cups cooked chickpeas

One 10-ounce package frozen chopped spinach, thawed and squeezed of excess liquid

¾ cup finely chopped red bell pepper

4 scallions, white and light green parts only, finely chopped

3 cloves garlic, minced

2 tablespoons finely chopped fresh flat-leaf parsley

½ teaspoon ground cumin

½ teaspoon ground turmeric

Sea salt

Freshly ground black pepper

3 large eggs, lightly beaten

1 cup panko bread crumbs, plus more as needed

4 tablespoons extra-virgin olive oil, plus more as needed

Sauce of your choice: such as Poblano Tahini Sauce (page 227), tahini, salsa, spiced yogurt

1. Preheat the oven to 350°F. Line a rimmed baking sheet with parchment paper and line another baking sheet with waxed paper.

2. In a stockpot fitted with a steamer basket, bring 2 inches of water to a simmer over medium-high heat. Place the cauliflower florets in the steamer, cover, and cook until just tender, 8 to 10 minutes.

3. Meanwhile, place the chickpeas into a large bowl and use a potato masher or fork to crush them. Add the cauliflower and mash until the ingredients are well smashed but not smooth. Add the spinach, bell pepper, scallions, garlic, and parsley and mix well. Stir in the cumin, turmeric, 1 teaspoon salt, and ¼ teaspoon black pepper. Add the eggs and ½ cup of the bread crumbs and stir to combine.

4. Place the remaining ½ cup bread crumbs in a shallow dish. Shape about ⅓ cup of the chickpea mixture into a patty ½ inch thick. Coat the patty lightly with bread crumbs. Place on the waxed paper–lined baking sheet. Repeat with the remaining mixture (to make 12 to 14 patties).

5. In a large nonstick skillet over medium heat, heat 2 tablespoons of the olive oil until shimmering. Place one-third to one-half of the patties in the pan and cook undisturbed until golden brown, about 4 minutes. Flip the patties and cook until golden, about 4 minutes more. Transfer the patties to the parchment-lined baking sheet. Wipe the skillet clean with paper towel. Repeat to cook the remaining patties, wiping the skillet clean and adding 2 tablespoons of oil before each batch. Transfer the patties to the baking sheet as they are done. When all the patties have been cooked, place the baking sheet in the oven and bake for 10 minutes.

6. Transfer the patties to a serving platter, season with additional salt and pepper, and serve hot, with the sauce passed separately.

From the Market

Cauliflower (1 small head)

Red bell pepper (1 medium)

Scallions (4)

Garlic (3 cloves)

Fresh flat-leaf parsley (1 small bunch)

Large eggs (3)

Frozen chopped spinach (one 10-ounce box)

Panko bread crumbs (1 cup, plus more as needed)

Sauce of your choice: such as Poblano Tahini Sauce (page 227), tahini, salsa, spiced yogurt

From the Pantry

Chickpeas (one 15-ounce can or 1½ cups cooked)

Extra-virgin olive oil (4 to 6 tablespoons)

Ground cumin (½ teaspoon)

Ground turmeric (½ teaspoon)

Sea salt

Black pepper

*You will need parchment paper.

Gluten-free: use gluten-free bread crumbs.

Perfect Paninis

4 SERVINGS   TIME: 15 MINUTES

In our family, we have a thing about sandwiches. No simple turkey, lettuce, and mayo on sandwich bread will do for us! We view sandwiches like any other recipe, building on ingredients and flavors to create a multi-layered taste sensation. Everyone has their own personal preferences, so instead of a specific recipe, here we offer a guide to assembling your own Perfect Panini.

1. Choose one from each category below:

FAT: 1 TABLESPOON, PLUS MORE AS NEEDED

Unsalted butter
Extra-virgin olive oil

KOSHER SALT

BREAD: 8 SLICES

Whole wheat
Multigrain
Sourdough
Country white
Ciabatta

CHEESE: 4 TO 8 OUNCES

Mozzarella
Provolone
Gruyère
Pepper Jack
Brie
Cheddar
Vegan cheese

SPREAD: 4 TABLESPOONS

Olive tapenade
Pesto
Quince paste (membrillo)
Guacamole
Mustard
Sriracha sauce

PROTEIN: 4 TO 8 OUNCES

Prosciutto
Cooked bacon or tempeh bacon
Cooked chicken
Seitan or seitan sausage

**VEGETABLES: 2 TO 4 OUNCES
(CHOOSE 1 TO 3 OPTIONS)**

Fresh basil leaves, very thinly sliced
(see chiffonade, page 26)
Baby arugula
Kimchi, drained
Sliced avocado
Pickled Red Onions (page 225)
Sliced pickles
Sliced jalapeño peppers
Sliced tomatoes

2. Using the bread, cheese, spread, protein, and vegetables of your choice, assemble 4 sandwiches, dividing the ingredients evenly among each.

3. In a large (preferably cast-iron) skillet over medium heat, melt the butter until it foams or heat the olive oil until shimmering and sprinkle the skillet with salt. Add the sandwiches to the skillet, in batches, if needed, and press firmly with the lid of a smaller pan or a grill press. Cook until golden brown, 3 to 4 minutes. Flip the sandwiches (adding 1 to 2 teaspoons more fat, if necessary) and cook until golden brown, an additional 3 to 4 minutes. Serve hot.

From the Market and Pantry

Unsalted butter or extra-virgin olive oil (1 tablespoon, plus more as needed)

Kosher salt

Bread
(8 slices)

Cheese
(4 to 8 ounces)

Spread (¼ cup)

Protein (4 to 8 ounces)

Vegetables (2 to 4 ounces)

Burgers, Patties, and Sandwiches   107

CHAPTER 6

Vegetable Mains

Healthy Vegetable-Fried Farro

4 SERVINGS TIME: 45 MINUTES

This dish is our take on fried rice, but here we've substituted farro—one of our favorite grains—for white rice. The chewy texture and nutty taste of the farro add complexity to this familiar dish. We've included traditional fried rice veggies like broccoli, carrots, and peas, but any assortment of vegetables you have on hand—like bell peppers, cauliflower, or spinach—will work. If you cook your farro the day before, this is a super-fast dish to get on the table.

2 cups farro

4 large eggs

2 tablespoons plus 1¼ teaspoons low-sodium soy sauce

2 teaspoons plus ¼ teaspoon toasted sesame oil

1 tablespoon plus 2 teaspoons peanut oil

1 cup sliced carrots, ¼-inch-thick rounds

2½ cups 1-inch broccoli florets

2 cloves garlic, minced

1 teaspoon grated fresh ginger

4 scallions, thinly sliced,
green and white parts separated

1 cup frozen petite peas, thawed

Kosher salt

½ teaspoon rice vinegar

Sriracha or chili garlic sauce (optional)

1. In a medium saucepan, cook the farro according to the directions on the package. Drain well and let cool. (The farro can be made ahead of time and refrigerated.)

2. In a small bowl, beat the eggs with ¼ teaspoon of the soy sauce and ¼ teaspoon of the sesame oil.

3. In a large nonstick skillet over medium-high heat, heat 1 teaspoon of the peanut oil until shimmering. Add the egg mixture and scramble until it sets, 3 to 4 minutes. Transfer the egg to a plate, cut into bite-size pieces, and set aside.

4. Wipe the skillet clean, add the remaining 1 tablespoon plus 1 teaspoon peanut oil, and heat over medium-high heat until shimmering. Add the carrots and cook, stirring, for 2 minutes. Add the broccoli and cook until the vegetables are fork-tender, 3 to 4 minutes. Stir in the garlic, ginger, scallion whites, and peas and cook for 2 minutes. Season with ½ teaspoon salt.

5. Using a wooden spoon, push the vegetables to the sides of the skillet, making a well in the center. Add the cooked farro to the well and gradually mix the vegetables into it.

6. Add the remaining 2 tablespoons plus 1 teaspoon soy sauce, the remaining 2 teaspoons sesame oil, and the vinegar. Stir in the scrambled eggs and mix well.

7. Serve hot, garnished with the scallion greens. Pass the Sriracha or chili garlic sauce separately, if desired.

From the Market

Broccoli (1 head)

Carrot (1 large)

Fresh ginger
(1-inch knob)

Scallions (4)

Garlic (2 cloves)

Large eggs (4)

Frozen petite peas
(1 cup)

From the Pantry

Farro (2 cups)

Low-sodium soy sauce
(2 tablespoons plus 1¼ teaspoons)

Toasted sesame oil
(2¼ teaspoons)

Peanut oil (1 tablespoon plus
2 teaspoons)

Kosher salt

Rice vinegar (½ teaspoon)

Sriracha or chili garlic sauce
(optional)

Buddha Bowl with Roasted Sweet Potatoes, Spiced Chickpeas, and Chard

4 SERVINGS TIME: 55 MINUTES

While Lori was in college in Northern California, we often went to visit. The food scene there had a big influence on all of us. Even those many years ago, we were into fresh, locally grown vegetables and whole grains. Our dog-eared cookbooks were *The Moosewood Cookbook* and *Laurel's Kitchen*. One of our favorite things to make in those days is what is now commonly referred to as Buddha bowls, which are composed of four elements: a grain, vegetables, a protein, and a sauce. Today we still love our Buddha bowls—so simple, nutrient-dense, and very pretty to serve.

FOR THE POBLANO TAHINI SAUCE

1½ cups roughly chopped poblano pepper

1 clove garlic, quartered

⅓ cup tahini (sesame paste)

3 tablespoons fresh lemon juice

1 tablespoon extra-virgin olive oil

Sea salt

Freshly ground black pepper

FOR THE BUDDHA BOWLS

1 cup quinoa, rice, or farro (or any grain of your choice)

2 large sweet potatoes (1½ to 2 pounds), peeled and cut into 1-inch cubes

1½ tablespoons coconut oil, melted

2 teaspoons pure maple syrup

1 teaspoon orange zest

Sea salt

One 15-ounce can chickpeas, drained, rinsed, and patted dry or 1½ cups cooked chickpeas

1 tablespoon plus 2 teaspoons extra-virgin olive oil

½ teaspoon paprika

⅛ teaspoon ground cumin

⅛ teaspoon cayenne pepper

Freshly ground black pepper

4 cloves garlic, peeled

⅛ teaspoon crushed red pepper flakes

1 bunch Swiss chard, red, green, or rainbow, stemmed, leaves cut into 1-inch strips

FOR THE POBLANO TAHINI SAUCE:

1. In a blender or food processor, combine the poblano, garlic, tahini, lemon juice, olive oil, and ¼ cup water and blend until smooth. (If the sauce is too thick, add water as needed to reach the desired consistency.) Season with ½ teaspoon salt and ⅛ teaspoon pepper. Set aside. (The dressing can be made ahead and stored in an airtight container in the refrigerator for up to 1 week.)

FOR THE BUDDHA BOWLS:

2. Preheat the oven to 425°F.

3. In a medium saucepan, cook the quinoa, rice, or farro according to the directions on the package.

4. In a medium bowl, combine the sweet potatoes, melted coconut oil, maple syrup, orange zest, and ¼ teaspoon salt. Mix well until the potatoes are evenly coated.

5. Spread the sweet potatoes on a rimmed baking sheet and roast for 20 minutes. Flip them with a spatula and roast until the potatoes are tender and beginning to brown, an additional 10 to 15 minutes.

Continued

Vegetable Mains   113

6. Meanwhile, in a small bowl, combine the chickpeas, 2 teaspoons of the olive oil, the paprika, cumin, cayenne, ¼ teaspoon salt, and ⅛ teaspoon pepper. Mix well until the chickpeas are thoroughly coated.

7. Spread the chickpeas on a rimmed baking sheet and roast with the sweet potatoes until golden brown, 15 to 20 minutes, stirring them once halfway through.

8. In a large skillet over medium-high heat, heat the remaining 1 tablespoon of the olive oil until shimmering. Add the garlic and red pepper flakes. Cook until the garlic is fragrant, 3 to

4 minutes. Add the chard, cover, and cook, stirring occasionally, until the chard begins to wilt, 2 to 3 minutes. Uncover, add ¼ teaspoon salt and ⅛ teaspoon pepper, and cook, stirring frequently, until the chard is completely wilted and cooked through, an additional 1 to 2 minutes. Discard the garlic cloves.

9. Put ½ cup of the cooked grain in the bottom of each of four serving bowls. Top each bowl with equal portions of the roasted sweet potatoes, roasted chickpeas, and sautéed chard. Drizzle with the poblano tahini sauce and serve with extra sauce passed separately.

From the Market
Swiss chard, red, green, or rainbow (1 bunch)
Sweet potatoes (2 large)
Poblano peppers (2 medium)
Garlic (5 cloves)
Orange (1)
Lemon (1)

From the Pantry
Quinoa, rice, farro, or any grain of your choice (1 cup)
Coconut oil (1½ tablespoons)
Maple syrup, pure (2 teaspoons)
Sea salt
Chickpeas (one 15-ounce can or 1½ cups cooked)
Tahini (⅓ cup)
Extra-virgin olive oil (2 tablespoons plus 2 teaspoons)

Paprika (½ teaspoon)
Ground cumin (⅛ teaspoon)
Cayenne pepper (⅛ teaspoon)
Black pepper
Crushed red pepper flakes (⅛ teaspoon)

Gluten-free: use quinoa or rice.

Vegan Thai Red Curry with Tofu and Vegetables

4 SERVINGS TIME: 1 HOUR 15 MINUTES

We love all different kinds of curries, but when we developed this recipe, we were in the mood for one with coconut milk. Having eaten tofu curry in restaurants all over New York City, we knew that the consistency of the tofu was crucial—we like it to be firm on the outside yet still moist and chewy. To achieve that texture, we looked to James Beard Award–winning author and chef Andrea Nguyen, a veritable tofu expert, and followed her preparation. Deep-frying it delivered the desired result and a perfect curry (you can also simply pan-fry the tofu, if you prefer).

One 14-ounce package firm organic tofu, drained

Kosher salt

2 cups boiling or very hot water

3 cups organic canola oil, or as needed

1 small Chinese eggplant, halved lengthwise and sliced into ¼-inch-thick half-moons

2 tablespoons low-sodium soy sauce

½ cup low-sodium vegetable broth

4 teaspoons turbinado sugar

One 13.5-ounce can unsweetened full-fat coconut milk (do not shake the can)

¼ cup red curry paste

10 small cremini mushrooms, stemmed and halved

1 small fresh red chile pepper, thinly sliced

1 small red bell pepper, sliced into strips

1 cup 1-inch broccoli florets

½ cup sliced bamboo shoots, drained and rinsed

⅓ cup chopped shallot

1 teaspoon minced fresh ginger

1 tablespoon fresh lime juice

10 fresh basil leaves, torn

2 cups cooked brown or white rice, for serving

1. Slice the tofu block in half horizontally to make 2 slabs. Cut each slab in half so you have 4 equal-size rectangles. Slice each rectangle in half to make 8 squares total. Finally, cut each square in half on the diagonal so you have 16 triangles. Place the tofu triangles in a shallow bowl. Dissolve 1 teaspoon salt in the boiling or very hot water and pour the water over the tofu. Set aside for 15 minutes.

2. Spread a tea towel over a rimmed baking sheet or line with paper towels.

3. Drain the tofu in a colander and set the triangles in a single layer on the prepared baking sheet. Cover with another towel (or paper towels) and place another baking sheet on top. Rest a weight (such as a small skillet) on the top baking sheet. Let the tofu drain for at least 15 minutes.

4. In a deep skillet or wok over high heat, heat ½ inch of the canola oil (use more or less oil as needed) until it registers 360°F on an instant-read thermometer. (Alternatively, insert the handle of a wooden spoon or a chopstick into the hot oil. If bubbles form around the wood and begin to float, the oil is ready.) Line a plate with paper towels and have it nearby.

Continued

5. Carefully add the tofu slices to the hot oil and cook until golden brown on the undersides, about 1 minute. Using chopsticks or a metal spatula, flip the tofu and cook for an additional minute, or until golden. Transfer to the paper towel–lined plate and set aside to drain. (The tofu can be prepared ahead and kept at room temperature, covered, for several hours, or stored in an airtight container in the refrigerator for up to 5 days; bring it to room temperature before using.)

6. Place the eggplant in a bowl with ½ teaspoon salt and toss to coat. Set aside for about 5 minutes, until the eggplant starts releasing liquid. Rinse the eggplant, carefully squeeze out any excess liquid, and set aside.

7. In a small bowl, stir together the soy sauce, broth, and sugar and set aside.

8. Open the can of coconut milk without shaking it. Spoon 5 to 6 tablespoons of the cream from the top into a wok or large skillet. Cook over medium-high heat until the coconut cream begins to bubble, about 1 minute. Add the curry paste and reduce the heat to medium-low. Cook, stirring, until the curry is fragrant, about 3 minutes. Add the eggplant, mushrooms, chile pepper, bell pepper, broccoli, bamboo shoots, shallot, and ginger. Raise the heat to medium and stir until the vegetables are coated and hot, 2 to 3 minutes. Add the remaining coconut milk and bring to a boil, then reduce the heat to low and cook until the vegetables are tender, 7 to 10 minutes.

9. Add the tofu and the soy sauce mixture, stir, and simmer for 2 minutes. Turn off the heat and add the lime juice and basil leaves. Season with salt.

10. Divide the curry among four individual bowls and serve with the rice.

From the Market

Organic tofu, firm
(one 14-ounce package)

Broccoli (1 small head)

Red bell pepper (1 small)

Chinese eggplant
(1 small or about 6 ounces)

Cremini (baby bella) mushrooms
(10 small)

Fresh red chile pepper (1 small)

Fresh ginger (1 small knob)

Shallot (1 large)

Fresh basil (1 small bunch)

Lime (1)

Coconut milk, unsweetened full-fat
(one 13.5-ounce can)

Red curry paste (¼ cup)

Bamboo shoots
(one 8-ounce can)

Cooked rice for serving (2 cups)

From the Pantry

Kosher salt

Organic canola oil (3 cups)

Low-sodium soy sauce
(2 tablespoons)

Low-sodium vegetable broth
(½ cup)

Turbinado sugar (4 teaspoons)

Gluten-free: use tamari in place of soy sauce.

Vegetarian Mapo Tofu with Spinach

Fragrant and spicy, our take on this Sichuan classic really packs a punch. Most *mapo tofu* recipes include pork, but we wanted a vegetarian alternative; the fermented black beans and the shiitake mushrooms add savory depth and texture so we don't miss the meat. It doesn't hurt that we can get this dish on the table in less than half an hour.

3 tablespoons vegetable oil

1½ tablespoons fermented black beans

3 dried red chile peppers
(½ teaspoon crushed red pepper flakes)

1 tablespoon chile bean sauce (*toban djan*)

1 tablespoon grated fresh ginger

2 cloves garlic, minced

2 cups sliced stemmed shiitake mushrooms

1 tablespoon low-sodium soy sauce

1 teaspoon toasted sesame oil

1 teaspoon rice vinegar

1 teaspoon ground Sichuan peppercorns
(if not available, use ¼ teaspoon freshly ground black pepper)

1½ cups low-sodium vegetable broth

One 14-ounce package soft organic tofu
(if not available, use medium-firm; do not use silken), drained between paper towels and cut into 1-inch cubes

1 tablespoon cornstarch, dissolved in
3 tablespoons cold water

2½ cups firmly packed baby spinach

4 scallions, thinly sliced,
green and white parts separated

8 to 12 Rice Noodle Nests (page 220), or cooked noodles or rice of your choice, for serving

1. In a wok or deep skillet over medium-high heat, heat the vegetable oil until shimmering. Add the fermented black beans, chile peppers, and chile bean sauce. Cook, stirring, for about 1 minute. Add the ginger and garlic and stir. Add the mushrooms, soy sauce, sesame oil, vinegar, and Sichuan peppercorns and mix well. Add the broth and cook, stirring, for 2 minutes.

2. Carefully add the tofu and gently mix with a wooden spoon. While stirring, slowly pour in the cornstarch mixture and stir to incorporate. Add the spinach and stir, then add the scallion whites and cook for 3 minutes more, or until the sauce is thick and glossy.

3. Place two Rice Noodle Nests (or a serving of cooked noodles or rice) into individual serving bowls, ladle the tofu on top, garnish with the scallion greens, and serve.

From the Market

Organic tofu, soft or medium-firm (not silken) (one 14-ounce package)

Baby spinach (5 ounces)

Shiitake mushrooms (6 ounces)

Ginger (1 knob)

Scallions (4)

Garlic (2 cloves)

Dried red chile peppers (3) or crushed red pepper flakes (½ teaspoon)

Fermented black beans (1½ tablespoons)

Chile bean sauce (*toban djan*) (1 tablespoon)

Ground Sichuan peppercorns (1 teaspoon) or if not available, use freshly ground black pepper (¼ teaspoon)

From the Pantry

Cornstarch (1 tablespoon)

Vegetable oil (3 tablespoons)

Low-sodium soy sauce (1 tablespoon)

Toasted sesame oil (1 teaspoon)

Rice vinegar (1 teaspoon)

Low-sodium vegetable broth (1½ cups)

Additional Ingredients

Rice Noodle Nests (page 220) or noodles or rice of your choice

Gluten-free: use tamari in place of soy sauce. Use gluten-free chile bean sauce.

Amped-Up Vegetable Nachos

4 TO 6 SERVINGS   TIME: 35 MINUTES

This dish comes out of the oven sizzling and bubbling and is devoured as soon as it hits the table. Everybody loves nachos, but it's not typically a dish that offers much in the way of nutrition. We've taken these up a notch by loading them with kale, corn, beans, and avocado. And yes, cheese, too. The end result is addictive.

2 tablespoons extra-virgin olive oil

1 cup chopped red onion

2 cloves garlic, minced

4 cups roughly chopped stemmed lacinato (dinosaur or Tuscan) kale leaves

Kosher salt

Freshly ground black pepper

1½ cups fresh or thawed frozen corn kernels

One 15-ounce can refried beans

2 tablespoons low-sodium vegetable broth

2 tablespoons Pico de Gallo (page 228) or your favorite store-bought salsa, plus more for serving

40 Tortilla Chips (page 224), or your favorite store-bought

2 cups freshly shredded Monterey Jack cheese

10 pickled jalapeño slices

1 cup diced ripe avocado

1. Preheat the oven to 375°F.

2. In a large nonstick skillet over medium-high heat, heat 1 tablespoon of the olive oil until shimmering. Add the onion and garlic and cook, stirring with a wooden spoon, until the onion is soft and translucent, about 3 minutes. Add the kale, ½ teaspoon salt, and ⅛ teaspoon pepper and cook, stirring, for 1½ minutes. Add the corn and cook for an additional 1½ minutes. Transfer to a bowl and set aside.

3. Wipe out the skillet with paper towels and return it to medium-high heat. Add the remaining 1 tablespoon olive oil and the refried beans and stir. Pour in the broth and mix until incorporated. Add the pico de gallo and stir to combine. Set aside.

4. Divide the tortilla chips between two 9 by 13-inch baking dishes. Spoon the beans over the chips in each baking dish. Top each with half the vegetables and sprinkle the cheese evenly over each. Scatter the jalapeño slices on top. Bake until the cheese is melted, about 7 minutes. Switch the oven to broil and broil until the cheese is golden and bubbling, 1 to 2 minutes.

5. Serve with additional pico de gallo and the avocado.

From the Market

Lacinato (dinosaur or Tuscan) kale (1 bunch)

Corn (3 medium ears fresh or 1½ cups frozen)

Avocado, ripe (1)

Red onion (1 medium)

Garlic (2 cloves)

Monterey Jack cheese (8 ounces)

Pico de Gallo (2 tablespoons, plus more for serving; page 228, or your favorite store-bought salsa)

Pickled jalapeño peppers (1 small jar)

Tortilla Chips (40 chips; page 224 or your favorite store-bought)

From the Pantry

Kosher salt

Black pepper

Extra-virgin olive oil (2 tablespoons)

Refried beans (one 15-ounce can)

Low-sodium vegetable broth (2 tablespoons)

Vegan/Dairy-free: use vegan cheese.

Sheet Pan Tacos with Crispy Brussels Sprouts

6 TO 8 SERVINGS   TIME: 1 HOUR 15 MINUTES

We developed dozens of vegetarian taco recipes, and these were by far our favorites. The meaty flavor of the quinoa and beans is fantastic with the crispy texture of the Brussels sprouts. These tacos are not only mouthwatering but packed full of protein as well. **See photo on page 120**

FOR THE TACOS

1 cup quinoa, rinsed

1 cup low-sodium vegetable broth

1½ pounds Brussels sprouts, trimmed and halved lengthwise or quartered, if large

3 tablespoons extra-virgin olive oil

Kosher salt

Freshly ground black pepper

1 tablespoon nutritional yeast

2 teaspoons chili powder

2 teaspoons ground cumin

1 teaspoon paprika

½ teaspoon garlic powder

¼ teaspoon cayenne pepper (optional)

1 cup canned black beans, drained and rinsed, or 1 cup cooked black beans

⅓ cup chopped shallot

½ cup Pico de Gallo (page 228) or your favorite store-bought salsa, plus more for serving

12 to 16 corn tortillas

FOR THE SRIRACHA MAYONNAISE

½ cup vegan mayonnaise

1 tablespoon Sriracha sauce

1½ teaspoons fresh lime juice

¼ teaspoon kosher salt

¼ teaspoon freshly ground black pepper

Pickled Red Onions (page 225) or
sliced pickled jalapeño peppers, for serving

FOR THE TACOS:

1. Preheat the oven to 425°F. Line a rimmed baking sheet with parchment paper.

2. In a medium saucepan over medium heat, toast the quinoa, stirring frequently, until lightly browned and fragrant, 3 to 5 minutes. Add the broth and ½ cup water. Raise the heat to high to bring to a boil. Reduce the heat to low, cover, and cook until the liquid has been absorbed, 15 to 20 minutes.

3. Meanwhile, in a large bowl, combine the Brussels sprouts, 2 tablespoons of the olive oil, ½ teaspoon salt, and ¼ teaspoon black pepper and mix well. Spread the Brussels sprouts over a rimmed baking sheet and roast for 15 minutes. Remove from the oven and set aside.

4. Reduce the oven temperature to 400°F.

5. In a large bowl, combine the nutritional yeast, chili powder, cumin, paprika, garlic powder, cayenne pepper (if using), ¼ teaspoon salt, and ¼ teaspoon black pepper. Mix well until blended. Add the cooked quinoa, black beans, shallot, pico de gallo, and remaining 1 tablespoon olive oil. Spread the quinoa mixture over the parchment-lined baking sheet. Roast for 15 minutes, then remove from the oven, flip the quinoa mixture with a spatula, and return both it and the baking sheet with the Brussels sprouts to the oven for an additional 15 minutes.

6. Wrap the tortillas in aluminum foil and place in the oven for 10 minutes before serving.

FOR THE SRIRACHA MAYONNAISE:

7. Combine all the Sriracha mayonnaise ingredients in a small bowl and mix well. Set aside.

8. Top each tortilla with three or four spoonfuls each of the quinoa and Brussels sprouts. Serve with additional pico de gallo, the Sriracha mayonnaise, and pickled red onions (or jalapeños).

From the Market

Brussels sprouts (1¼ pounds)

Shallots (2 large)

Lime (1)

Corn tortillas (12 to 16)

Pico de Gallo (½ cup, plus more for serving; page 228, or your favorite store-bought salsa)

Pickled Red Onions (page 225) or jalapeño peppers (1 small jar)

From the Pantry

Quinoa (1 cup)

Low-sodium vegetable broth (1 cup)

Extra-virgin olive oil (3 tablespoons)

Kosher salt

Black pepper

Nutritional yeast (1 tablespoon)

Chili powder (2 teaspoons)

Ground cumin (2 teaspoons)

Paprika (1 teaspoon)

Garlic powder (½ teaspoon)

Cayenne pepper (¼ teaspoon; optional)

Black beans (one 15-ounce can or 1 cup cooked)

Vegan mayonnaise (½ cup)

Sriracha sauce (1 tablespoon)

*You will need parchment paper.

Linguine with Spinach and Golden Garlic Bread Crumbs

4 TO 6 SERVINGS   TIME: 25 MINUTES

Swiss chard and kale have become so popular that we sometimes forget our earlier love: spinach, that nutrient powerhouse. In this ultra-easy dish, we sauté spinach with garlic, add linguine, and then sprinkle toasted garlicky bread crumbs on top. This is a super-quick weeknight meal that both adults and kids enjoy.

Kosher salt

½ cup plus 2 tablespoons extra-virgin olive oil

6 cloves garlic: 1 minced, 5 thinly sliced

¾ cup panko bread crumbs

Freshly ground black pepper

1 pound linguine

¼ teaspoon crushed red pepper flakes, or to taste

1 pound baby spinach

½ cup plus 2 tablespoons freshly grated Parmesan cheese

1. Bring a large pot of water to a boil over high heat and add 1 tablespoon salt.

2. Meanwhile, in a large skillet over medium heat, heat 2 tablespoons of the olive oil. Add the minced garlic and cook, stirring, for about 30 seconds. Add the bread crumbs and cook, stirring frequently, until golden, 2 to 3 minutes. Season with salt and pepper. Remove from the heat and set aside.

3. Cook the pasta in the boiling water until al dente, about 2 minutes less than the directions on the package. Reserve ½ cup of the pasta water and drain the pasta in a colander.

4. Wipe out the skillet, set it over medium heat, and add the remaining ½ cup olive oil. Add the sliced garlic and the red pepper flakes and cook, stirring frequently, until the garlic is very lightly browned, 3 to 4 minutes.

5. Slowly add the spinach and cook, using tongs to mix it thoroughly with the oil, until wilted, 2 to 3 minutes. Pour in the reserved pasta water and mix well. Add the cooked linguine and ½ cup of the cheese and use the tongs to thoroughly combine. Season with ½ teaspoon salt and ⅛ teaspoon black pepper. Add ¼ cup of the bread crumbs and toss.

6. Transfer the pasta to a serving bowl, sprinkle with the remaining bread crumbs and remaining 2 tablespoons cheese, and serve hot.

From the Market
Linguine (1 pound)
Baby spinach (1 pound)
Garlic (6 cloves)
Parmesan cheese (3 ounces)

From the Pantry
Kosher salt
Extra-virgin olive oil (½ cup plus 2 tablespoons)
Panko bread crumbs (¾ cup)

Black pepper
Crushed red pepper flakes (¼ teaspoon)

Vegan/Dairy-free: omit the cheese.

Penne with Roasted Vegetables and Mozzarella

6 TO 8 SERVINGS   TIME: 1 HOUR

During the hot summer months, sweet and succulent heirloom tomatoes are bountiful. We like to hit up our local farmer's market and buy handfuls of them for this homemade tomato sauce. To preserve that off-the-vine flavor, we use a box grater to grate the tomatoes directly into the skillet. The result is an incredibly sweet and garden-fresh sauce.

1¼ pounds eggplant, cut into 1-inch cubes (6 cups)

Kosher salt

1 Cubanelle or Italian pepper, halved lengthwise, seeded, and thinly sliced into half-moons

5 tablespoons extra-virgin olive oil

Freshly ground black pepper

4 cups diced zucchini, cut into 1-inch cubes

1 pound penne pasta

2 pounds ripe heirloom tomatoes, halved horizontally

3 cloves garlic, minced

½ teaspoon crushed red pepper flakes, or to taste

1 cup diced fresh mozzarella cheese, cut into ¼-inch cubes

¼ cup fresh basil, very thinly sliced (see chiffonade, page 26)

¼ cup freshly grated Parmesan cheese

1. Set the racks in the upper and lower thirds of the oven and preheat the oven to 425°F. Line two rimmed baking sheets with parchment paper.

2. Place the eggplant in a strainer and sprinkle with 1½ teaspoons salt. Set the strainer in the sink for 20 minutes, then rinse and pat dry the eggplant with paper towels. Transfer the eggplant to a large bowl and add the Cubanelle pepper, 3 tablespoons of the olive oil, and ⅛ teaspoon black pepper. Using your hands, toss the eggplant and pepper in the oil, making sure they are well coated. Spread them in a single layer on one of the prepared baking sheets.

3. Spread the zucchini over the second prepared baking sheet. Drizzle with 1 tablespoon of the olive oil and season with ½ teaspoon salt and ⅛ teaspoon black pepper. Use your hands to toss until well coated, then spread the zucchini back into a single layer over the baking sheet.

4. Place both baking sheets in the oven, with the eggplant on the lower rack and the zucchini on the upper rack. Roast for 20 minutes, or until browned, then remove from the oven. Flip the vegetables with a spatula and return the baking sheets to the oven, switching their positions (upper rack and lower rack). Roast for an additional 5 minutes, then remove the zucchini from the oven and roast the eggplant for 5 minutes more. Remove from the oven.

5. Meanwhile, bring a large pot of water to a boil. Add 1 tablespoon salt and the pasta. Cook until al dente, about 1 minute less than the directions on the package. Drain the pasta in a colander. Set aside.

6. Working over a large skillet, hold one tomato half, cut-side out in the palm of one hand and a box grater in the other. Grate the tomato on the large holes of the box grater so the pulp falls into the skillet. Discard the skin and repeat with the remaining tomato halves.

7. Add the remaining 1 tablespoon olive oil, the garlic, and red pepper flakes to the tomatoes and bring to a simmer over low heat. Cook until the tomato pulp has reduced by half, 20 to 25 minutes. Add 1 teaspoon salt, the cooked pasta, and the roasted eggplant and zucchini, and stir until incorporated.

8. Transfer the pasta to a serving bowl and add the mozzarella and basil. Sprinkle with the Parmesan cheese and serve hot.

From the Market
Penne pasta (1 pound)
Eggplant (1¼ pounds)
Zucchini (2 small)
Cubanelle or Italian pepper (1)
Ripe heirloom tomatoes (2 pounds)
Garlic (3 cloves)

Fresh basil (1 bunch)
Fresh mozzarella cheese (6 ounces)
Parmesan cheese (1 ounce)

From the Pantry
Kosher salt
Extra-virgin olive oil
(5 tablespoons)

Black pepper
Crushed red pepper flakes
(½ teaspoon)

*You will need parchment paper.

Cavatappi with Broccolini, Brown Butter, and Sage

4 TO 6 SERVINGS   TIME: 30 MINUTES

This pasta dish comes together quickly and easily, but doesn't fall short on flavor. Fragrant sage combines with butter and Parmesan to create a luscious sauce, which complements the crunchy Broccolini. We prefer to use Broccolini because it is sweeter, but feel free to substitute any type of broccoli.

Kosher salt

2 bunches Broccolini (about 1 pound), ends trimmed, split lengthwise into halves or thirds depending on the thickness (or substitute broccoli rabe or broccoli)

2 tablespoons extra-virgin olive oil

2 large cloves garlic, minced

¼ teaspoon crushed red pepper flakes

Freshly ground black pepper

1 pound cavatappi pasta
(or your favorite ribbed pasta)

6 tablespoons unsalted butter, cubed

15 fresh sage leaves, torn

½ cup freshly grated Parmesan cheese

1. Bring a large pot of water to a boil. Fill a large bowl with water and ice and set aside.

2. Add 1 tablespoon kosher salt and the Broccolini to the boiling water and cook until crisp-tender, 2 to 3 minutes. Using a spider or slotted spoon, transfer the Broccolini to the ice water to stop the cooking and let cool. Keep the pot of water boiling for the pasta. Drain the Broccolini in a colander, cut the stalks in half crosswise, and set aside.

3. In a large nonstick skillet over medium heat, heat the olive oil until shimmering. Add the garlic and red pepper flakes and cook, stirring frequently, for 1 minute. Add the blanched Broccolini, ½ teaspoon salt, and ¼ teaspoon black pepper and sauté until tender, 3 to 5 minutes. Transfer the Broccolini to a medium bowl and set aside.

4. Add the pasta to the boiling water and cook until al dente, about 2 minutes less than the directions on the package. Reserve ½ cup of the pasta water and drain the pasta in a colander.

5. Meanwhile, wipe out the skillet, return it to medium-low heat, and add the butter. When the butter has melted, add the sage leaves and cook until the butter turns amber brown and the sage shrivels, 4 to 6 minutes. Add ¼ teaspoon salt and ⅛ teaspoon black pepper. Stir in the cooked pasta until incorporated, then fold in the Broccolini and 2 to 3 tablespoons of the reserved pasta water.

6. Stir in the Parmesan cheese, adding more pasta water until you achieve desired creaminess. Season with salt and pepper and serve hot.

From the Market

Cavatappi or ribbed pasta
(1 pound)

Broccolini, broccoli rabe, or broccoli
(2 bunches or about 1 pound)

Fresh sage leaves (15)

Garlic (2 large cloves)

Parmesan cheese (2 ounces)

Unsalted butter (6 tablespoons)

From the Pantry

Kosher salt

Extra-virgin olive oil
(2 tablespoons)

Crushed red pepper flakes
(¼ teaspoon)

Black pepper

Bucatini with Sautéed Chard and Vegetarian Sausage

4 TO 6 SERVINGS TIME: 40 MINUTES

We love a pasta dish that's loaded with vegetables, and we love chard—Swiss, red, green, or rainbow, we don't care. It has such a zesty, slightly salty flavor, which makes it an ideal ingredient for pastas. This dish can be modified for lots of tastes and diets—you can easily make it vegan, or dairy-free, or substitute meat sausage for the veggie. We like to make it vegetarian—it's one of those meatless dishes that has a lot of appeal to meat-eaters; they don't feel like they're missing anything in terms of taste and texture.

¼ cup plus 1 tablespoon extra-virgin olive oil

3 precooked vegetarian Italian sausages, sliced into ½-inch-thick rounds

Kosher salt

1 pound bucatini (or spaghetti)

2 large bunches Swiss chard (red, green, rainbow, or a combination), stemmed, tender stems chopped into ½-inch pieces (discard the thicker part of the stems), leaves roughly chopped

4 cloves garlic, sliced

⅛ teaspoon crushed red pepper flakes, or to taste

3 tablespoons chopped fresh flat-leaf parsley

Freshly ground black pepper

¼ cup freshly grated Parmesan cheese (optional)

1. Bring a large pot of water to a boil over high heat.

2. Meanwhile, in a large nonstick skillet over medium-high heat, heat 1 tablespoon of the olive oil until shimmering. Add the sausage slices in one layer and cook undisturbed until browned, 2 to 4 minutes. Using tongs, flip the sausage and cook until browned, an additional 2 to 4 minutes. Transfer the sausage to a plate and set aside.

3. Add 1 tablespoon salt and the pasta to the boiling water and cook until al dente, about 2 minutes less than the directions on the package. Reserve ¼ cup of the pasta water and drain the pasta in a colander.

4. In the same skillet you used for the sausage, heat the remaining ¼ cup olive oil over medium heat until shimmering. Add the chard stems and sauté until they begin to soften, 3 to 5 minutes. Stir in the garlic, red pepper flakes, and 2 tablespoons of the parsley and cook for 3 minutes. Add the chard leaves in bunches and sauté until wilted, 5 to 7 minutes. (You can cover the skillet with a large lid to quicken the process, but continue to stir often.) Once wilted, mix in the sausage and season with ½ teaspoon salt and ⅛ teaspoon black pepper.

Continued

5. Add the cooked pasta and 3 to 4 tablespoons of the reserved pasta water and cook, stirring, until the pasta is well coated, about 3 minutes.

6. Transfer the pasta to a serving bowl and sprinkle with the remaining 1 tablespoon parsley and the Parmesan cheese, if desired. Season with salt and pepper and serve hot.

Food for Thought

Along with kale and spinach, chard is predominant among the healthiest of the leafy green vegetables. It is a leading vegetable source of vitamin K, which benefits bone, heart, and cognitive health—in fact, 1 cup of chard has three times the daily recommended intake. To top it all off, the biotin found in chard helps stimulate the growth of healthy, strong hair!

From the Market
Precooked vegetarian Italian sausages (3 links, about 9 ounces)
Bucatini or spaghetti (1 pound)
Swiss chard, red, green, or rainbow (2 large bunches)
Garlic (4 cloves)

Fresh flat-leaf parsley (1 small bunch)
Parmesan cheese (1 ounce)

From the Pantry
Extra-virgin olive oil (¼ cup plus 1 tablespoon)
Kosher salt

Black pepper
Crushed red pepper flakes (⅛ teaspoon)

Vegan/Dairy-free: omit the Parmesan cheese.

Vegan Lentil and Roasted Tomato Pasta

4 TO 6 SERVINGS TIME: 1 HOUR 10 MINUTES

This hearty pasta dish includes green lentils for a protein-packed meal. Roasted plum tomatoes add sweetness and color, and lots of vegetables make this dish super healthy and pleasingly delicious.

¼ cup plus 2 tablespoons extra-virgin olive oil

1 cup finely chopped yellow onion

½ cup finely chopped carrot

½ cup finely chopped red bell pepper

⅓ cup finely chopped celery

1¼ cups green lentils, rinsed

4 cups low-sodium vegetable broth

5 plum tomatoes, halved

Kosher salt

Freshly ground black pepper

2 cloves garlic, minced

1 pound spaghetti

12 ounces baby spinach

¼ teaspoon crushed red pepper flakes, or to taste

⅓ cup fresh basil, very thinly sliced
(see chiffonade, page 26)

1. Preheat the oven to 450°F.

2. In a large saucepan over medium-high heat, heat ¼ cup of the olive oil until shimmering. Add the onion, carrot, bell pepper, and celery and sauté until lightly browned, about 10 minutes. Add the lentils, broth, and 1 cup water and stir. Bring to a boil, then reduce the heat to low and simmer until the lentils are just tender, 35 to 40 minutes.

Transfer to a large bowl and set aside. Wipe out the pan.

3. Place 1 tablespoon of the olive oil in a baking dish. Add the tomatoes, cut-side up, and sprinkle with ¼ teaspoon salt, ⅛ teaspoon black pepper, and the garlic. Roast until lightly browned, 30 to 35 minutes. Remove from the oven and set aside.

4. Bring a large pot of water to a boil over high heat. Add 1 tablespoon salt and the pasta. Cook until al dente, about 2 minutes less than the directions on the package. Drain the pasta in a colander.

5. In the same pan you used for the lentils, heat the remaining tablespoon of olive oil over medium heat until shimmering. Add the spinach and sauté until wilted, 2 to 3 minutes. Add the tomatoes and their juices and stir well, about 1 minute. Add the lentil mixture and cook, stirring for an additional 3 to 4 minutes, until the lentils are tender.

6. Raise the heat to high. Add the cooked spaghetti, stir to combine, and cook for 1 minute. Add ½ teaspoon salt, ⅛ teaspoon black pepper, the red pepper flakes, and the basil and mix well. Serve hot.

From the Market
Spaghetti (1 pound)
Plum tomatoes (5 ripe)
Carrot (1 small)
Celery (1 stalk)
Red bell pepper (1 small)
Baby spinach (12 ounces)

Yellow onion (1 small)
Garlic (2 cloves)
Fresh basil (1 small bunch)

From the Pantry
Extra-virgin olive oil
(¼ cup plus 2 tablespoons)
Green lentils (1¼ cups)

Low-sodium vegetable broth (1 quart)
Kosher salt
Black pepper
Crushed red pepper flakes
(¼ teaspoon)

Crispy Kale and Potato Hash with Fried Eggs

4 SERVINGS TIME: 1 HOUR 10 MINUTES

Sometimes you just want breakfast for dinner, and the combination of potato hash and eggs never disappoints. In our *Mostly Plants*—style hash, we add roasted kale for extra nutrition and a nice element of crunch. This light, simple, and tasty hash is comfort food at its best!

1½ pounds small white or red potatoes, cut into ½-inch cubes

1 tablespoon white or apple cider vinegar

Sea salt

1 medium yellow onion, halved and thinly sliced into half-moons

3 cloves garlic, thinly sliced

2 tablespoons chopped fresh flat-leaf parsley

1 teaspoon chopped fresh thyme, plus 4 or 5 sprigs

Freshly ground black pepper

4 to 5 tablespoons extra-virgin olive oil

4 cups packed curly kale, completely dry, stemmed and torn into 2-inch pieces

4 to 8 large eggs, room temperature

Crushed red pepper flakes (optional)

1. Preheat the oven to 425°F. Line two rimmed baking sheets with parchment paper.

2. Place the potatoes in a medium pot and add water to cover. Add the vinegar (this helps the potato pieces keep their shape) and 1 teaspoon salt. Cover the pot and bring the water to a boil. Reduce the heat to medium-high, set the lid ajar, and cook until the potatoes are fork-tender, 5 to 7 minutes. Drain well.

3. In a large bowl, combine the potatoes, onion, and garlic. Add the parsley, chopped thyme, 1½ teaspoons salt, ¼ teaspoon black pepper, and 2 tablespoons of the olive oil. Toss to coat thoroughly.

4. Arrange the potato mixture in a single layer on one of the prepared baking sheets. Scatter the thyme sprigs on top. Roast the potatoes undisturbed until the bottoms are golden brown, 25 to 30 minutes, then flip and roast until golden brown, an additional 15 to 20 minutes.

5. Meanwhile, place the kale in a large bowl and add 1 tablespoon of the olive oil. Using your fingers, massage the oil into the leaves well (do not add salt yet, as it draws out moisture and the leaves won't crisp in the oven).

6. Arrange the kale in a single layer on the second prepared baking sheet. Roast with the potatoes until browned and crisp, about 15 minutes, flipping once halfway through. Remove from the oven, season with salt to taste, and set aside.

7. In a large nonstick skillet over medium heat, heat the remaining olive oil until shimmering (use 1 tablespoon if making 4 eggs, 2 tablespoons if making 8 eggs). One at a time, crack the eggs into the skillet. Cook until the whites are set and the yolks are at your desired runniness, 3 to 5 minutes.

8. Discard the thyme sprigs from the potato hash. Spoon a generous serving of the hash onto individual serving plates. Top each with one-quarter of the roasted kale and finish with 1 or 2 fried eggs. Season with salt and black pepper, sprinkle with red pepper flakes, if desired, and serve.

From the Market

Curly kale (1 large bunch)

Small white or red potatoes
(1½ pounds)

Yellow onion (1 medium)

Garlic (3 cloves)

Fresh flat-leaf parsley (1 small bunch)

Fresh thyme (1 small bunch)

Large eggs (4 to 8)

From the Pantry

White or apple cider vinegar
(1 tablespoon)

Sea salt

Black pepper

Extra-virgin olive oil
(4 to 5 tablespoons)

Crushed red pepper flakes (optional)

*You will need parchment paper.

Rainbow Frittata

4 SERVINGS TIME: 35 MINUTES

Frittatas are one of those dishes that are perfect for any meal—we make them for breakfast, lunch, and dinner, or serve them thinly sliced as an appetizer when entertaining. They taste just as good at room temperature as they do hot out of the oven. They are so easy to prepare—you need just one skillet, and the filling options are endless. Most important tip: For the filling, stick to ingredients that are already cooked—too much moisture will make the frittata soggy.

1 tablespoon plus 1 teaspoon extra-virgin olive oil

1 cup finely chopped yellow onion

1 cup thinly sliced stemmed cremini mushrooms

1 cup diced red bell pepper, cut into ½-inch pieces

1 cup sliced zucchini, cut into ¼-inch-thick rounds

Kosher salt

Freshly ground black pepper

8 large eggs

⅓ cup whole milk

¾ cup shredded Gruyère cheese

1. Preheat the oven to 350°F.

2. In a 10-inch ovenproof skillet over medium-low heat, heat the olive oil until shimmering. Add the onion and sauté until translucent, about 4 minutes. Add the mushrooms and cook until they have softened and released most of their liquid, 4 to 5 minutes. Stir in the bell pepper and cook for 1 minute. Add the zucchini and cook for an additional 3 minutes, or until the zucchini begins to soften. Add ¼ teaspoon salt and ⅛ teaspoon black pepper and stir.

3. Meanwhile, whisk the eggs just enough to combine the whites and yolks (overbeating will cause the frittata to fall). Add ½ teaspoon salt and ¼ teaspoon black pepper. Add the milk and ½ cup of the cheese and gently stir to combine.

4. Pour the egg mixture over the vegetables in the skillet, covering them evenly. Cook the frittata, without stirring, until its edges start to set and curl away from the pan, about 5 minutes.

5. Place the skillet in the oven and bake for 15 to 18 minutes, until just puffed and set (be careful not to overcook it). Remove from the oven, sprinkle the remaining ¼ cup cheese evenly over the top, and bake for an additional 2 minutes. Switch the oven to broil and broil for 1 to 2 minutes, until the cheese is lightly golden.

6. Slice the frittata into wedges and serve.

From the Market

Zucchini (1 medium)

Red bell pepper (1 large)

Cremini (baby bella) mushrooms (4 ounces or 6 to 8 mushrooms)

Yellow onion (1 medium)

Large eggs (8)

Whole milk (⅓ cup)

Gruyère cheese (3 ounces)

From the Pantry

Extra-virgin olive oil (1 tablespoon plus 1 teaspoon)

Kosher salt

Black pepper

Three Greens Spanakopita Casserole

8 SERVINGS TIME: 1 HOUR 20 MINUTES

We took the classic "spinach pie" and really upped the vegetable ante by adding chard and kale. The luscious greens combined with the tangy feta cheese and flaky phyllo crust create a mouth watering casserole. Serve with a salad for dinner or cut into bite-size pieces for a fabulous hors d'oeuvre.

FOR THE FILLING

4 tablespoons extra-virgin olive oil

1 bunch Swiss chard, stemmed and cut into 1-inch pieces

2¼ cups tightly packed baby kale

2 pounds baby spinach

1 cup chopped yellow onion

1 shallot, diced

3 cloves garlic, minced

¼ cup chopped fresh flat-leaf parsley

2 tablespoons minced fresh dill

Kosher salt

Freshly ground black pepper

2 cups crumbled good-quality feta cheese (about 12 ounces)

4 large eggs, beaten

1 teaspoon lemon zest

Juice of 1 lemon

FOR THE PHYLLO CRUST

6 tablespoons unsalted butter

3 tablespoons olive oil, plus more for greasing

5 fresh sage leaves

20 sheets from 1 box of phyllo dough, defrosted in the refrigerator

1. Preheat the oven to 375°F.

FOR THE FILLING:

2. In a large skillet over medium heat, heat 1 tablespoon of the olive oil until shimmering. Add the chard and cook, stirring, until wilted, 1 to 2 minutes. Add the kale and sauté until fully wilted, 3 to 4 minutes. Transfer to a colander to drain.

3. Return the skillet to the stove over medium heat and add 1 tablespoon of the olive oil. When the oil is shimmering, add the spinach in batches and cook until wilted, 3 to 5 minutes. Transfer the spinach to the colander with the other greens and, using the back of a wooden spoon, press out the excess liquid. Set aside.

4. Wipe out the skillet, return it to medium-high heat, and add the remaining 2 tablespoons olive oil. Once the oil is shimmering, add the onion and cook, stirring, until translucent, 3 to 4 minutes. Add the shallot and cook for 3 minutes. Add the garlic and stir for 30 seconds, then return the greens to the skillet and stir well. Add the dill and parsley and cook, stirring to incorporate, for 2 minutes.

5. Remove the skillet from the heat, season lightly with salt and pepper, and set aside.

6. In a large bowl, combine the feta cheese, beaten eggs, lemon zest, lemon juice, ¼ teaspoon salt,

Continued

and ¼ teaspoon pepper. Add the sautéed greens and mix well until completely incorporated.

FOR THE PHYLLO CRUST:

7. In a small saucepan over medium heat, melt the butter with the olive oil. Add the sage leaves and simmer for 3 minutes. Remove from the heat and set aside to let the sage infuse the butter mixture.

8. Grease a 9 by 13-inch baking dish with olive oil. Tear off a large sheet of parchment paper or waxed paper and moisten a large kitchen towel or several paper towels.

9. Remove the phyllo dough from its wrapper and unroll it on a clean, dry cutting board or work surface. Remove 1 phyllo sheet and set aside, immediately covering the remaining sheets with the parchment or waxed paper and placing the moist towel (or paper towels) on top to prevent them from drying out. Place the first phyllo sheet in the prepared baking dish so that one long side is running down the center of the dish and the other is draped over the side.

10. Place a second sheet of phyllo on the other long side of the baking dish (the sheets should overlap in the center). Arrange 2 more sheets so they overhang the short sides of the baking dish. Using a pastry brush, spread a light layer of the sage butter all over the phyllo surface, including the overhanging sides. Repeat twice more, using 4 sheets for each layer and brushing butter over each (you will have used 12 sheets).

11. Lay 1 sheet of phyllo and rest it over the phyllo on the bottom of the dish and brush with butter.

12. Pour in the filling and smooth it with a spatula, spreading it to the sides and into the corners of the dish. Fold the overhanging phyllo over the filling and brush them with butter. One at a time, layer 7 more phyllo sheets lengthwise over the filling, tucking the edges into the sides and brushing each sheet with butter before adding the next. Brush the top sheet with butter.

13. Using your hands (a piece of waxed paper works great here), gently press down on the pie to compress the layers and remove any air pockets. With a sharp knife, gently score the top phyllo layers into 8 servings, making sure not to cut through to the filling.

14. Bake until golden brown and crisp, 35 to 45 minutes. Serve hot.

THE EXTRA PHYLLO CAN BE ROLLED IN WAX PAPER, THEN WRAPPED IN PLASTIC WRAP AND REFRIGERATED FOR UP TO 3 DAYS.

From the Market

Frozen phyllo dough (one 16-ounce box)

Swiss chard (1 bunch)

Baby spinach (2 pounds)

Baby kale (8 ounces)

Yellow onion (1 medium)

Shallot (1 medium)

Garlic (3 cloves)

Fresh flat-leaf parsley (1 small bunch)

Fresh dill (1 small bunch)

Fresh sage (1 small bunch)

Lemon (1)

Feta cheese, good-quality (2 cups, about 12 ounces)

Large eggs (4)

Unsalted butter (6 tablespoons)

From the Pantry

Extra-virgin olive oil (7 tablespoons, plus more for greasing)

Kosher salt

Black pepper

*You will need parchment paper.

Orecchiette with Shaved Brussels Sprouts and Creamy Parsley Pesto

4 TO 6 SERVINGS TIME: 40 MINUTES

Growing up, we weren't huge fans of Brussels sprouts—they were often boiled and flavorless (sorry, Mom!). Over the years we have gotten much more creative in how we cook vegetables, in terms of bringing out their best, and Brussels sprouts fall into this category. Now they are one of our staples. In this dish, we shred them into thin strips and then sauté them until they caramelize, bringing out their sweet and nutty flavor. The Brussels sprouts, combined with the orecchiette and creamy parsley pesto, make a vibrant, tasty, and satisfying meal.

FOR THE PESTO

2 cups tightly packed fresh flat-leaf parsley leaves

¾ cup extra-virgin olive oil

¼ cup plus 2 tablespoons chopped raw walnuts

2 cloves garlic, lightly crushed

Kosher salt

Freshly ground black pepper

½ cup plus 2 tablespoons freshly grated Parmesan cheese

FOR THE PASTA

Kosher salt

1 pound orecchiette pasta

1 pound Brussels sprouts, trimmed

2 tablespoons extra-virgin olive oil

2 large cloves garlic, minced

¼ teaspoon crushed red pepper flakes

Freshly ground black pepper

3 tablespoons heavy cream

1. Bring a large pot of water to a boil.

FOR THE PESTO:

2. In a food processor or blender, combine the parsley, olive oil, walnuts, garlic, ¾ teaspoon salt, and ⅛ teaspoon black pepper. Pulse until coarsely chopped. Scrape down the sides with a rubber spatula, add the Parmesan cheese, and pulse again until smooth and evenly blended, 1 to 2 minutes. Transfer to a small bowl and set aside.

FOR THE PASTA:

3. Add 1 tablespoon salt and the pasta to the boiling water and cook until al dente, about 1 minute less than the directions on the package. Reserve ½ cup of the pasta water and drain the pasta in a colander.

4. While the pasta cooks, clean the food processor bowl, if you used it for the pesto, and fit the food processor with the slicing blade. Use the processor to thinly slice the Brussels sprouts. (Alternatively, use a sharp knife to thinly slice them.) Set aside.

5. In a large nonstick skillet over medium heat, heat the olive oil until shimmering. Add the garlic and red pepper flakes and cook, stirring frequently and taking care not to burn the garlic,

Continued

for 2 minutes. Add the Brussels sprouts, ½ teaspoon salt, and ¼ teaspoon black pepper and sauté until the sprouts begin to soften, about 3 minutes. Spread the sprouts in the skillet and press down on them with the back of a wooden spoon to flatten. Cook undisturbed for 1 to 2 minutes to brown them, then stir and repeat. Turn off the heat and set aside.

6. In a separate large skillet over low heat, heat the heavy cream for about 30 seconds, then add 1 cup of the pesto (or to taste) and stir well to incorporate. Stir in the cooked pasta. Once incorporated, add the Brussels sprouts and mix well. Add 2 to 3 tablespoons of the reserved pasta water, for desired creaminess. Season with salt and black pepper and serve hot.

Food for Thought

Don't discard that sprig of parsley on your plate! While parsley is typically thought of as a garnish, it is actually a super-healthy herb. Initially used as a medicinal plant, parsley is filled with the flavonoid myricetin, which helps prevent cancer and protect against diabetes. It is also loaded with vitamin K and helps protect against osteoporosis.

From the Market
Orecchiette pasta (1 pound)
Brussels sprouts (1 pound)
Fresh flat-leaf parsley (2 bunches)
Garlic (4 cloves)
Heavy cream (3 tablespoons)
Parmesan cheese (3 ounces)

From the Pantry
Extra-virgin olive oil
(¾ cup plus 2 tablespoons)
Raw walnuts
(¼ cup plus 2 tablespoons)
Crushed red pepper flakes
(¼ teaspoon)

Kosher salt
Black pepper

Sheet Pan Vegetable and Tofu Dinner

4 SERVINGS   TIME: 55 MINUTES

One reason we love sheet pan recipes is that cleanup is a breeze. In this vegetarian sheet pan meal, we add bite-size cubes of tofu along with lots of vegetables. The dish is finished with a combination of cheeses melted over the top for a gooey and wonderful result.

One 14-ounce package extra-firm organic tofu, drained

12 ounces assorted baby potatoes (about 12), cut into quarters lengthwise

2 medium carrots, cut into 1-inch pieces

3 tablespoons extra-virgin olive oil

Kosher salt

Freshly ground black pepper

4 cups 1½-inch broccoli florets

3 cups 1½-inch cauliflower florets

1 tablespoon unsalted butter

2 tablespoons finely chopped shallot

1 clove garlic, minced

¼ cup dry white wine

½ cup low-sodium vegetable broth

½ teaspoon low-sodium soy sauce

½ cup firmly packed shredded cheddar cheese

½ cup firmly packed shredded Monterey Jack cheese

1. Preheat the oven to 425°F. Line a rimmed baking sheet with parchment paper.

2. Line a plate with several paper towels and place the tofu on top. Cover the tofu with a few more paper towels. Place another dinner plate on top and rest a weight (such as a book or heavy can) on the plate. Let the tofu drain for at least 10 minutes and up to 1 hour.

3. In a medium bowl, combine the potatoes, carrots, 1 tablespoon of the olive oil, 1 teaspoon salt, and ⅛ teaspoon pepper. Mix well until the vegetables are evenly coated. Spread them in a single layer on the prepared baking sheet, making sure not to crowd them or they will steam. Roast for 20 minutes.

4. Meanwhile, cut the tofu into 1-inch cubes. Place the tofu in a medium bowl and add 2 teaspoons of the olive oil, ½ teaspoon salt, and ⅛ teaspoon pepper. Gently mix until well coated and set aside.

5. In a separate medium bowl, combine the broccoli, the cauliflower, the remaining 1 tablespoon plus 1 teaspoon olive oil, ½ teaspoon salt, and ⅛ teaspoon pepper. Mix well until the vegetables are evenly coated. Spread them in a single layer on a second unlined baking sheet, making sure not to crowd them. Set aside.

6. Remove the potatoes and carrots from the oven, flip them, and move them closer together, leaving one-third of the baking sheet free for the

tofu. Arrange the tofu on the baking sheet and return it to the oven. Roast for 20 minutes.

7. Place the broccoli and cauliflower in the oven with the other vegetables and the tofu and roast for 20 to 22 minutes, until beginning to brown, flipping halfway through.

8. While the vegetables are roasting, in a small saucepan over medium heat, melt the butter. Add the shallot and garlic and cook, stirring, until the shallot becomes translucent, about 4 minutes. Add the wine and cook for 2 minutes. Stir in the broth and soy sauce and season with pepper. Bring to a boil, then reduce the heat to low and simmer for 10 minutes, stirring occasionally.

9. Remove the baking sheets from the oven. Using a spatula, transfer the potatoes, carrots, and tofu on top of of the broccoli and cauliflower. Spoon the sauce over all the vegetables and sprinkle the cheeses evenly over the top. Return to the oven and bake for 5 to 7 minutes more, until the cheese has melted. Switch the oven to broil and broil for 2 to 3 minutes, until the cheese is bubbling. Plate and serve hot.

From the Market

Extra-firm organic tofu
(one 14-ounce package)

Assorted baby potatoes
(12 ounces or about 12)

Carrots (2 medium)

Broccoli (1 large head)

Cauliflower (1 head)

Shallots (2 small)

Garlic (1 clove)

Unsalted butter (1 tablespoon)

Cheddar cheese (4 ounces)

Monterey Jack cheese (4 ounces)

From the Pantry

Extra-virgin olive oil
(3 tablespoons)

Kosher salt

Black pepper

Dry white wine (¼ cup)

Low-sodium vegetable broth
(½ cup)

Low-sodium soy sauce
(½ teaspoon)

*You will need parchment paper.

 (GF)

Gluten-free: use tamari in place of soy sauce.

Heavenly Meatless Meatballs
with Quick Tomato Sauce

6 SERVINGS (THIRTY 1½-INCH MEATBALLS)   TIME: 2 HOURS

These meatless meatballs satiate even the most ardent of carnivores. You can actually make vegetarian meatballs from almost any combination of vegetable, grain, and legume, but this mix is our all-time favorite. We love serving these veggie meatballs over pasta or in a hero topped with melted cheese, but they can also hold their own with a side of cauliflower rice or broccoli rice.

FOR THE SAUCE

2 tablespoons extra-virgin olive oil

2 cloves garlic, minced

¼ teaspoon crushed red pepper flakes

2 tablespoons tomato paste

Two 28-ounce cans crushed tomatoes

6 fresh basil leaves

Kosher salt

Freshly ground black pepper

2 tablespoons unsalted butter, cubed

1 teaspoon light brown sugar

FOR THE MEATBALLS

½ cup plus 2 tablespoons French lentils, rinsed

1 bay leaf

3 tablespoons extra-virgin olive oil

1 large yellow onion, chopped

2 carrots, chopped

2 celery stalks, chopped

1 clove garlic, minced

Kosher salt

3 tablespoons tomato paste

1 cup chopped cremini mushrooms, stemmed

½ cup canned chickpeas, drained and rinsed, or ½ cup cooked chickpeas

½ cup quick-cooking rolled oats

½ cup chopped fresh flat-leaf parsley

¼ cup chopped fresh basil

Freshly ground black pepper

2 large eggs, beaten

½ cup plain bread crumbs

½ cup freshly grated Parmesan cheese, plus more for serving

FOR THE SAUCE:

1. In a large saucepan over medium heat, heat the olive oil until shimmering. Add the garlic and red pepper flakes and sauté until the garlic is fragrant, about 1 minute. Add the tomato paste and cook, stirring, until the paste has blended with the oil and darkened slightly, about 2 minutes.

2. Add the crushed tomatoes, raise the heat to medium-high, and bring to a simmer. Add the basil leaves, 1 teaspoon salt, and ¼ teaspoon black pepper and reduce the heat to low. Simmer for 20 minutes, or until the sauce has reduced slightly. Add the butter and brown sugar and stir to combine. Season with salt and black pepper. (The sauce can be made ahead and stored in an airtight container in the refrigerator for up to 5 days or in the freezer for up to 6 months. Reheat the sauce before adding the meatballs.)

FOR THE MEATBALLS:

3. In a medium saucepan, combine the lentils, bay leaf, and 2 quarts water and bring to a boil.

Continued

Reduce the heat to low and simmer until the lentils are soft but not falling apart, 20 to 25 minutes. Discard the bay leaf. Drain the lentils and let cool.

4. In a large nonstick skillet over medium-high heat, heat 2 tablespoons of the olive oil until shimmering. Add the onion, carrots, celery, garlic, and ½ teaspoon salt. Sauté for 7 to 10 minutes, until the vegetables are tender and beginning to brown.

5. Add the tomato paste and cook, stirring, for 2 to 3 minutes, until the vegetables are evenly coated. Add the mushrooms and cook, stirring frequently, for an additional 5 minutes.

6. Transfer the vegetable mixture to a large food processor. Add the cooked lentils, chickpeas, oats, parsley, basil, ½ teaspoon salt, and ¼ teaspoon pepper and pulse until combined (you want a coarse, not mushy, consistency), scraping down the sides of the bowl several times. Transfer the mixture to a large bowl and add the eggs, bread crumbs, and Parmesan cheese. Mix by hand until fully incorporated. Refrigerate the meatball mixture for 30 minutes.

7. Preheat the oven to 400°F. Grease a large rimmed baking sheet evenly with the remaining 1 tablespoon olive oil.

8. Using your hands, roll the meatball mixture into about thirty 1½-inch balls, using about 3 tablespoons of the mixture for each. Place the meatballs on the prepared sheet, making sure to leave space between each one. Bake for 30 minutes, or until firm and lightly browned.

9. Return the sauce to a simmer. Remove the meatballs from the oven and add them to the sauce.

10. Serve the meatballs and sauce as you like, with additional Parmesan cheese sprinkled on top, if desired.

From the Market
Carrots (2 medium)
Celery (2 stalks)
Cremini (baby bella) mushrooms
(4 ounces or 6 to 8 mushrooms)
Yellow onion (1 large)
Garlic (3 cloves)
Fresh basil (1 bunch)
Fresh flat-leaf parsley (1 bunch)
Unsalted butter (2 tablespoons)
Parmesan cheese
(2½ ounces)

Large eggs (2)
Rolled oats, quick-cooking (½ cup)

From the Pantry
Extra-virgin olive oil
(5 tablespoons)
Crushed red pepper flakes
(¼ teaspoon)
Tomato paste (5 tablespoons)
Crushed tomatoes
(two 28-ounce cans)
Kosher salt

Black pepper
Light brown sugar (1 teaspoon)
French lentils
(½ cup plus 2 tablespoons)
Bay leaf (1)
Chickpeas (½ cup canned or cooked)
Plain bread crumbs (½ cup)
*You will need parchment paper.

Gluten-free: use gluten-free bread crumbs and oats.

Teriyaki Tempeh with Broccolini and Carrots

4 SERVINGS TIME: 30 MINUTES

Three great reasons why we love this dish: It's super healthy, super quick to get on the table, and super delicious. Tempeh, with its firm, dense texture and lovely earthy flavor, is a wonderful substitute for meat. And tempeh is so good for you, with loads of protein, fiber, and B vitamins, plus all the probiotic benefits of being a fermented food. This is a great weeknight dinner that everyone will love.

1 cup rice or quinoa

2 bunches Broccolini, ends trimmed, stalks sliced in half lengthwise

2 carrots, cut on an angle into ½-inch-thick slices

2 tablespoons peanut, grapeseed, or extra-virgin olive oil

Two 8-ounce packages organic tempeh, cut crosswise into ½-inch-thick slices

3 tablespoons Teriyaki Sauce (page 229) or your favorite store-bought teriyaki sauce, plus more to taste

1. Cook the rice or quinoa according to the directions on the package and set aside.

2. Meanwhile, in a medium saucepan, blanch the Broccolini and carrots until crisp-tender, about 3 minutes (see page 129 for instructions). Drain in a colander and set aside.

3. In a large nonstick skillet over medium-high heat, heat 1 tablespoon of the oil until shimmering. Place the tempeh slices in the pan and cook undisturbed until browned, 3 to 4 minutes. Flip the tempeh (we like using tongs for this), add the remaining 1 tablespoon oil, and cook until browned, an additional 3 to 4 minutes.

4. Add the blanched vegetables to the skillet and gently mix with the tempeh. Add the 3 tablespoons of teriyaki sauce and stir well to coat. Add additional teriyaki sauce, if desired. Cook, stirring, until hot, 3 to 4 minutes.

5. Spoon ½ cup of the cooked grains into each of four serving bowls. Top each bowl with the tempeh and vegetables and serve hot.

From the Market
Organic tempeh (two 8-ounce packages)
Broccolini (2 bunches)
Carrots (2 medium)
Teriyaki Sauce (¼ cup; page 229, or your favorite store-bought)

From the Pantry
Rice or quinoa (1 cup)
Peanut, grapeseed, or extra-virgin olive oil (2 tablespoons)

Gluten-free: use gluten-free teriyaki sauce.

CHAPTER 7

Seafood Mains

Salmon Piccata with Wilted Spinach and Navy Beans

4 SERVINGS TIME: 30 MINUTES

In this revamp of the classic Italian piccata, salmon stands in for the veal. All the unmistakable piccata flavors are still here—tangy lemon, pungent garlic, and briny capers, bound together in a velvety, buttery sauce. We've upped the plant quotient by adding nutrient-rich spinach and protein-packed navy beans.

Four 6-ounce skinless salmon fillets

Kosher salt

Freshly ground black pepper

1 tablespoon extra-virgin olive oil

2 cloves garlic, minced

8 cups tightly packed baby spinach

One 15-ounce can navy beans, drained and rinsed, or 1½ cups cooked navy beans

2 tablespoons grapeseed oil

3 tablespoons finely chopped shallot

1 cup low-sodium vegetable broth

¼ cup dry white wine

2 tablespoons fresh lemon juice

2 tablespoons capers, drained

3 tablespoons unsalted butter, cubed

3 tablespoons finely chopped fresh flat-leaf parsley

4 lemon slices, for serving (optional)

1. Season each fillet with salt and pepper.

2. In a large nonstick skillet over medium heat, heat the olive oil. Add the garlic and cook, stirring, for 1 minute, or until fragrant. Slowly add the spinach and cook, stirring, until wilted, 2 to 3 minutes. Add the beans and season with salt and pepper. Mix until combined. Cook until the beans are warm, about 2 minutes, and remove from the heat.

3. In a separate large nonstick skillet over medium-high heat, heat the grapeseed oil until shimmering. Gently add the fillets to the pan and cook for 3 to 4 minutes on each side, until light golden brown. Transfer the fillets to a platter and tent with aluminum foil to keep warm.

4. Add the shallot to the hot skillet and cook, stirring, until translucent, about 1 minute. Add the broth, wine, lemon juice, and capers. Cook, stirring occasionally, until the liquid has reduced slightly, 4 to 5 minutes. Add the butter and, when melted, add 2 tablespoons of the parsley and stir.

5. Distribute the sautéed spinach and beans among four individual plates. Top each with a salmon fillet and spoon the sauce over each one. Sprinkle with the remaining 1 tablespoon parsley and top with a lemon slice, if desired. Serve hot.

Food for Thought

Spinach is one of the most nutritious leafy greens there is—it ranks at or near the top of the list as a source of magnesium, iron, and vitamins B2, B6, and K. Spinach is also an excellent source of potassium—more so than even bananas—which helps improve blood pressure, heart and bone health, and cognitive function. What's more, spinach is loaded with the most protein of the leafy greens—over 5 grams in 1 cup cooked.

From the Market

Salmon
(four 6-ounce skinless fillets)

Baby spinach (10 ounces)

Shallots (3 small)

Garlic (2 cloves)

Fresh flat-leaf parsley
(1 small bunch)

Lemons (2)

Unsalted butter (3 tablespoons)

From the Pantry

Kosher salt

Black pepper

Extra-virgin olive oil
(1 tablespoon)

Navy beans (one 15-ounce can
or 1½ cups cooked)

Grapeseed oil (2 tablespoons)

Low-sodium vegetable broth (1 cup)

Dry white wine (¼ cup)

Capers (2 tablespoons)

Mediterranean Sea Bass

4 SERVINGS TIME: 35 MINUTES

Sea bass has a light, moist texture, so we like to briefly pan-sear it and finish it quickly in the oven. We then smother the fish in a piquant, healthy, Mediterranean-inspired sauce made from tomatoes, white wine, fennel, and olives. This dish takes 35 minutes from start to finish, so it's ideal for weeknight suppers yet elegant enough for company.

FOR THE SAUCE

2 tablespoons extra-virgin olive oil

1 cup chopped yellow onion

3 cloves garlic, minced

¼ teaspoon crushed red pepper flakes, or to taste

½ cup chopped fennel

One 28-ounce can whole peeled tomatoes, with their juices

¾ cup fresh basil leaves, very thinly sliced (see chiffonade, page 26)

½ cup dry white wine

¼ cup pitted Kalamata olives, halved

Kosher salt

Freshly ground black pepper

FOR THE FISH

Four 4- to 6-ounce skinless Chilean sea bass fillets (or other sustainable firm white-fleshed fish fillets)

Organic olive oil cooking spray

Kosher salt

Freshly ground black pepper

1 tablespoon extra-virgin olive oil

1. Set the racks in the middle and upper thirds of the oven and preheat the oven to 425°F.

FOR THE SAUCE:

2. In a large skillet over medium heat, heat the olive oil until shimmering. Add the onion, garlic, and red pepper flakes and cook until golden, stirring occasionally, about 5 minutes. Add the fennel and cook until the vegetables are soft and translucent, an additional 3 to 5 minutes.

3. Reduce the heat to medium and add the tomatoes with their juices. Using the back of a wooden spoon, smash the tomatoes and cook for 5 minutes. Add the basil, wine, olives, 1 teaspoon salt, and ⅛ teaspoon black pepper. Reduce the heat to low and simmer for 15 minutes, or until the sauce is slightly thickened, while you prepare the fish.

FOR THE FISH:

4. Pat the fillets dry, lightly spray them with cooking spray, and season with salt and pepper.

5. In a heavy ovenproof skillet over high heat, heat the olive oil until shimmering. Add the fillets, rounded-side down, and cook for 2 minutes. Carefully flip the fillets with a metal spatula and place the skillet in the oven. Bake until the fish is no longer translucent, 8 to 10 minutes.

6. Switch the oven to broil and place the skillet on the upper rack. Broil until the tops of the fillets are golden brown, 2 to 4 minutes.

7. Arrange the fillets on individual plates, spoon on the sauce, and serve.

From the Market

Chilean sea bass or other
sustainable firm white-fleshed fish
(four 4- to 6-ounce skinless fillets)

Fennel (1 small bulb)

Yellow onion (1 small)

Garlic (3 cloves)

Fresh basil (1 small bunch)

Kalamata olives, pitted
(¼ cup)

From the Pantry

Extra-virgin olive oil (3 tablespoons)

Crushed red pepper flakes
(¼ teaspoon)

Whole peeled tomatoes
(one 28-ounce can)

Dry white wine (½ cup)

Organic olive oil cooking spray

Kosher salt

Black pepper

Martha's Vineyard Seafood and Chicken Paella

6 TO 8 SERVINGS   TIME: 1 HOUR 45 MINUTES

Don't be put off by the number of ingredients and the many steps in this recipe—it's all worth it. This paella, with its play of colors and flavor intensity, is fabulous for special occasions and feeding a crowd. We often brown the chicken and chorizo and steam the lobster, mussels, and clams early in the day, then put them aside in the refrigerator. Forty minutes before hungry eaters arrive, we cook the rice, add the prepared ingredients, and the paella is ready.

FOR THE SEAFOOD

1 dozen littleneck clams, well scrubbed

½ cup dry white wine

1 dozen mussels, well scrubbed

Two 1¼-pound lobsters

FOR THE PAELLA

6 small bone-in, skin-on chicken thighs

Sea salt

Freshly ground black pepper

4 tablespoons extra-virgin olive oil

One ½-pound fresh uncured (Mexican) chorizo link, cut into ½-inch-thick rounds

1 large Spanish onion, chopped

6 cloves garlic, minced and mashed with a bit of salt

¼ teaspoon crushed red pepper flakes, or to taste

2 cups Bomba rice (if not available, use Arborio rice)

5 cups low-sodium chicken broth

2 teaspoons smoked paprika

½ teaspoon saffron threads, crumbled

FOR THE SEAFOOD:

1. Place the clams and ¼ cup of the wine in a medium saucepan over medium-high heat. Cover tightly and cook for 3 to 5 minutes, just until the clams open. Using a slotted spoon, transfer the clams to a bowl (keeping them in their shells), discarding any that have not opened. Pour the cooking liquid into a bowl and let cool.

2. Put the mussels and remaining ¼ cup wine in the same pan over medium-high heat. Cover tightly and cook for 3 to 5 minutes, just until the mussels open. Transfer the mussels to the bowl with the clams (keeping them in their shells), discarding any that have not opened; set the clams and mussels aside. Pour the cooking liquid into the bowl with the clam cooking liquid.

3. Line a sieve with cheesecloth or a paper towel and set it over a bowl. Strain the clam and mussel liquid through the lined sieve to get rid of any grit. Set aside.

4. Bring 2 inches of water to a simmer in a lobster pot. Add the lobsters and quickly cover the pot. Steam the lobsters until the shells are bright red, about 10 minutes. Remove the lobsters from the pot with tongs and let cool 5 minutes. Split the lobster tails in half, crack the claws, and set aside. (Reserve the bodies for later use or discard.)

FOR THE PAELLA:

5. Set a rack in the lowest third of the oven and preheat the oven to 400°F.

6. Pat the chicken dry and liberally season with salt and pepper.

7. In a 15-inch paella pan over medium-high heat, heat 2 tablespoons of the olive oil until shimmering. Add the chorizo and cook for 2 to

Continued

3 minutes, until lightly browned. Flip and cook on the other side until lightly browned, an additional 1 to 2 minutes. Transfer the chorizo to a bowl. Do not wipe the pan.

8. Add the onion to the pan and cook, stirring occasionally, until they are tender and golden, 4 to 5 minutes. Add the garlic and red pepper flakes and cook, stirring to combine, for an additional minute. Turn off the heat and transfer the onion mixture to a bowl. Do not wipe the pan.

9. In the same pan over medium-high heat, heat the remaining 2 tablespoons olive oil. When shimmering, add the chicken, skin-side down, and cook until lightly browned, about 5 minutes. Flip and cook for an additional 4 minutes, until lightly browned. Transfer the chicken to a plate (it will finish cooking in the rice). Do not wipe the pan.

10. Add the rice to the pan and cook over medium-high heat, stirring continuously, until browned, 4 to 5 minutes. Stir in the broth, ½ cup of the

reserved clam and mussel liquid, the smoked paprika, saffron, ½ teaspoon salt, and ⅛ teaspoon black pepper and bring to a boil over high heat. Rotate the pan occasionally, but do not stir the rice. Continue cooking until the broth bubbles and the rice floats to the surface of the pan, 12 to 14 minutes. (A spoon pulled through the rice should leave a path.) Reduce the heat to medium, add the chicken to the rice, and nestle in the chorizo, onion, and clams and mussels in their shells.

11. Place the pan on the lowest rack of the oven and bake until the liquid has been absorbed and a crust (called the *socarrat*) begins to appear around the edges of the pan, 10 to 12 minutes (the rice should still be a bit al dente). Remove the pan from the oven, nestle in the lobster tails and claws, and return to the oven for an additional 5 minutes. Remove the pan from the oven, let the paella rest for 5 minutes, and serve.

Littleneck clams (12)
Mussels (12)
Lobsters (two, 1¼ pounds each)
Fresh uncured (Mexican) chorizo (1 link, about ½ pound)
Chicken thighs (6 small, bone-in, skin-on)
Spanish onion (1 large)

Garlic (6 cloves)
Saffron (½ teaspoon)
Bomba rice (3 cups) or if not available, use Arborio rice

From the Pantry
Dry white wine (½ cup)
Extra-virgin olive oil (¼ cup)

Crushed red pepper flakes (¼ teaspoon)
Smoked paprika (2 teaspoons)
Sea salt
Black pepper
Low-sodium chicken broth (5 cups)

Shrimp Scampi with Zucchini Noodles

4 SERVINGS   TIME: 35 MINUTES

Zucchini noodles are an ideal gluten-free alternative to pasta. Zucchini has a mild flavor and a similar texture to linguine, so we find it is the ultimate partner to this lemony, garlicky sauce with seared shrimp. This is a lighter, healthier alternative to an old Italian standard.

1 pound large shrimp (31/35 count), peeled, deveined, and butterflied

Kosher salt

¼ teaspoon baking soda

4 medium zucchini (about 2 pounds), or 2 pounds store-bought zucchini noodles

5 tablespoons extra-virgin olive oil, plus more as needed

1 tablespoon minced garlic

1 small fresh red chile pepper (such as cayenne or Thai bird), thinly sliced

2 teaspoons capers, drained

½ cup dry vermouth or dry white wine

3 tablespoons unsalted butter

1 teaspoon lemon zest

1 tablespoon fresh lemon juice

1 teaspoon chopped fresh flat-leaf parsley

1 teaspoon chopped fresh tarragon

Freshly ground black pepper

1. In a medium bowl, combine the shrimp, ½ teaspoon salt, and the baking soda. Mix well until evenly coated. Set aside at room temperature for 10 minutes or refrigerate for up to 1 hour.

2. Cut the zucchini into noodles using a vegetable spiralizer, according to the manufacturer's directions. Place the spiralized zucchini in a bowl lined with paper towel or a tea towel to remove any excess water.

3. In a large skillet over medium-high heat, heat 2 tablespoons of the olive oil until shimmering. Add half the shrimp in one layer, cut-side down with the tails sticking up, and cook undisturbed until pink, 1½ to 2 minutes. Flip and cook, turning and stirring the shrimp occasionally, for an additional 2 minutes. Transfer the shrimp to a medium bowl. Repeat with the remaining shrimp, adding more oil to the pan if needed. Set aside.

4. Wipe the skillet clean, return it to medium heat, and add 1 tablespoon of the olive oil, the garlic, and chile pepper. Cook, stirring, until the garlic starts to turn golden brown, about 1 minute. Add the capers and cook for an additional minute, making sure the garlic doesn't burn.

5. Add the vermouth, raise the heat to high, and stir until the liquid has reduced by half, about 3 minutes. Add the butter and stir until melted. Remove from the heat and stir in the lemon zest, lemon juice, parsley, tarragon, ½ teaspoon salt,

Continued

and ⅛ teaspoon black pepper. Pour the sauce over the shrimp and toss until well coated; set aside.

6. Wipe the skillet clean, return it to medium-high heat, and add the remaining 2 tablespoons of olive oil. When the oil is very hot, add the zucchini noodles and cook, stirring continuously, for 2 minutes. Transfer the shrimp and all of the sauce to the skillet, mix into the zucchini, and cook for an additional minute. Season with salt and black pepper. Transfer to a serving bowl and serve hot.

Food for Thought

Who knew zucchini was a great choice for those looking to lose a few pounds? It's high in water and low in calories, as well as rich in vitamins C, A, and K. Zucchini is also brimming with nutrients like potassium and manganese. Oh, and remember not to peel it—the skin is an excellent source of fiber.

From the Market

Shrimp, large (1 pound, 31/35 count)

Zucchini (4 medium) or zucchini noodles (2 pounds)

Fresh red chile pepper, cayenne or Thai bird (1 small)

Garlic (2 cloves)

Fresh flat-leaf parsley (1 small bunch)

Fresh tarragon (2 sprigs)

Lemon (1)

Unsalted butter (3 tablespoons)

From the Pantry

Kosher salt

Baking soda (¼ teaspoon)

Extra-virgin olive oil (¼ cup plus 1 tablespoon)

Capers (2 teaspoons)

Dry vermouth or dry white wine (½ cup)

Black pepper

Asian Parchment Parcels with Salmon or Tofu

4 SERVINGS   TIME: 1 HOUR

Baking in parchment is one of the healthiest and easiest ways to prepare fish. In this dish, the fish and vegetables steam together in a flavorful marinade. The results are delightfully moist fish and crisp, tender vegetables.

FOR THE SAUCE

¼ cup dry white wine

¼ cup low-sodium soy sauce

1 tablespoon fresh lime juice

1 tablespoon minced garlic

1 tablespoon mirin

1 tablespoon toasted sesame oil

1 tablespoon warm water

2 teaspoons minced fresh ginger

2 teaspoons rice vinegar

1 teaspoon light brown sugar

1 teaspoon sambal oelek

1 teaspoon sesame seeds

FOR THE PARCELS

8 ounces udon noodles

Organic olive oil cooking spray

Four 6-ounce skinless salmon fillets
(or two 12- to 14-ounce packages extra-firm organic tofu, drained and cut into 1-inch cubes)

Kosher salt

Freshly ground black pepper

8 baby bok choy, thinly sliced lengthwise
(if not available, use 2 regular bok choy)

4 medium carrots, cut on an angle into ¼-inch-thick slices

1 small head broccoli, cut into 1-inch florets

4 tablespoons roughly chopped fresh cilantro

1. Preheat the oven to 400°F. Tear off four 14- to 15-inch-long pieces of parchment paper. Fold each piece in half and cut into a half circle (to form a full circle when open).

FOR THE SAUCE:

2. Place all the sauce ingredients in a small bowl and whisk to combine. Set aside.

FOR THE PARCELS:

3. Bring a large pot of water to a boil. Add the udon noodles and cook until very al dente, about 4 minutes. Drain and rinse under cold water and place in a medium bowl. Add 2 tablespoons of the sauce and mix well.

4. If using tofu, place it in a medium bowl, add 1 to 2 tablespoons of the sauce, and stir to combine.

5. Spray one side of a parchment circle with cooking spray. Place one-quarter of the udon noodles in the center. Place a salmon fillet or tofu cubes on top of the noodles and season with salt and pepper. Top with one-quarter each of the bok choy, carrots, broccoli, and cilantro and 3 tablespoons of the sauce. Bring the edges of the parchment together to form a half circle and, working from one end, fold and crimp the edges to seal. Repeat with the remaining parchment and ingredients.

6. Arrange the pouches on two rimmed baking sheets. Bake until the parchment puffs up, 15 to 20 minutes.

7. Serve the pouches on individual plates. Open carefully to let the steam escape.

From the Market

Salmon (four 6-ounce skinless fillets) or extra-firm organic tofu (two 12- to 14-ounce packages)

Baby bok choy (8) or if not available, use regular bok choy (2)

Carrots (4 medium)

Broccoli (1 small head)

Fresh cilantro (1 small bunch)

Fresh ginger (1 small knob)

Garlic (2 large cloves)

Lime (1)

Sambal oelek (1 teaspoon)

From the Pantry

Dry white wine (¼ cup)

Low-sodium soy sauce (¼ cup)

Mirin (1 tablespoon)

Toasted sesame oil (1 tablespoon)

Rice vinegar (2 teaspoons)

Light brown sugar (1 teaspoon)

Sesame seeds (1 teaspoon)

Udon noodles (one 8-ounce package)

Organic olive oil cooking spray

Kosher salt

Black pepper

*You will need parchment paper.

Vegetarian/vegan: use tofu.
Vegan: use turbinado sugar in place of brown sugar.

Salmon Farro Bowl

4 SERVINGS TIME: 45 MINUTES

We first had this addicting salmon bowl with Vietnamese nuoc cham at Axe, a beloved restaurant in Venice, California, that has since closed. We were never able to get the recipe, but we have done our best to replicate its deliciousness, while substituting protein-packed farro for the brown rice in the original.

FOR THE SALMON AND FARRO

2 tablespoons low-sodium soy sauce

1 tablespoon mirin

1 tablespoon rice vinegar

1 tablespoon toasted sesame oil

1 tablespoon avocado oil, extra-virgin olive oil, or coconut oil

Four 6-ounce skinless salmon fillets

2 cups low-sodium vegetable broth

Kosher salt

1½ cups farro, rinsed and drained

FOR THE VIETNAMESE NUOC CHAM

2 tablespoons sugar

2½ teaspoons fresh lime juice

2 tablespoons Asian fish sauce

1 clove garlic, minced

1 fresh red Thai chile, seeded and thinly sliced (optional)

FOR THE BOWLS

1 tablespoon avocado oil, extra-virgin olive oil, or coconut oil

1 cup shredded red cabbage

2 medium carrots, cut into thin matchsticks

1 small Persian cucumber, sliced into ribbons

1 cup soybean sprouts

½ cup chopped fresh cilantro

½ cup chopped fresh mint

½ cup chopped fresh basil

4 tablespoons chopped roasted peanuts

FOR THE SALMON AND FARRO:

1. In a wide shallow dish, mix the soy sauce, mirin, vinegar, sesame oil, and avocado oil. Place the salmon fillets in the marinade and turn once, coating both sides. Cover and refrigerate for at least 20 minutes and up to 1 hour.

2. Set a rack in the middle of the oven and preheat the oven to 400°F.

3. In a medium saucepan, combine the broth and 1 cup water and bring to a boil. Add ½ teaspoon salt and the farro, cover the pan, reduce the heat to medium-low, and simmer for 20 to 25 minutes, until the water has been absorbed.

FOR THE VIETNAMESE NUOC CHAM:

4. In a small saucepan, combine the sugar, 1 tablespoon water, and ½ teaspoon of the lime juice. Heat over medium heat, stirring, until the sugar has dissolved, about 1 minute. Cook, stirring continuously, until the mixture thickens to the consistency of corn syrup, 3 to 5 minutes. Remove from the heat, pour the liquid into a small bowl, and add the remaining 2 teaspoons lime juice, the fish sauce, garlic, and Thai chile (if using). Mix well and set aside.

FOR THE BOWLS:

5. In a large ovenproof nonstick skillet over medium-high heat, heat the avocado oil until shimmering. Lay the salmon in the pan, rounded-side down, and cook undisturbed until a nice

Continued

brown crust forms, about 3 minutes. Carefully flip the fillets to the other side and place the skillet in the oven. Bake for 3 to 5 minutes for a rare center or 6 to 7 minutes for well done. Remove the skillet from the oven.

6. Divide the farro evenly among four serving bowls. Lay a salmon fillet on top of each mound of farro. Divide all the vegetables and herbs evenly and place them around the salmon. Pour some nuoc cham over each serving, making sure to coat the farro, salmon, and vegetables. Top each bowl with 1 tablespoon of the peanuts and serve.

Food for Thought

Salmon, considered a "super food," is one of the best sources of omega-3 fatty acids, an important nutrient for cognitive function, boosting memory, and slowing cognitive decline. Omega-3s also support heart health. In fact, research suggests that consuming two servings of salmon a week can improve cardiovascular health and lower your risk of heart failure.

From the Market

Salmon
(four 6-ounce skinless fillets)

Red cabbage
(4 ounces or 1 small head)

Carrots (2 medium)

Persian cucumber (1 small)

Soybean sprouts (4 ounces)

Fresh red Thai chile
(1; optional)

Garlic (1 clove)

Fresh cilantro (1 bunch)

Fresh mint (1 bunch)

Fresh basil (1 bunch)

Lime (1)

Roasted peanuts (¼ cup)

Avocado oil, extra-virgin olive oil or coconut oil (2 tablespoons)

From the Pantry

Low-sodium soy sauce
(2 tablespoons)

Mirin (1 tablespoon)

Rice vinegar (1 tablespoon)

Toasted sesame oil
(1 tablespoon)

Low-sodium vegetable broth
(2 cups)

Kosher salt

Farro (1½ cups)

Granulated sugar
(2 tablespoons)

Asian fish sauce
(2 tablespoons)

Shrimp and Kale Hot Pot

4 SERVINGS   TIME: 35 MINUTES

In this warming soup, sweet and succulent shrimp float in a fragrant broth. We lightly sauté the shrimp and the vegetables, then toss in an abundance of nutrient-rich baby kale, shiitake mushrooms, and rice vermicelli noodles and brighten it all with a spritz of lime.

4 ounces rice vermicelli noodles

Boiling water

3 tablespoons extra-virgin olive oil

¾ pound large shrimp (15/20 count), peeled and deveined

2 cups sliced stemmed shiitake mushrooms

¾ cup coarsely grated carrots

4 cloves garlic, thinly sliced

2 tablespoons finely chopped fresh ginger

4 cups low-sodium vegetable broth

3 tablespoons low-sodium soy sauce

Kosher salt

Freshly ground black pepper

2 cups tightly packed baby kale

2 teaspoons rice vinegar

2 teaspoons toasted sesame oil

1 small fresh red hot chile pepper, sliced, or to taste

1 bunch scallions, white and light green parts only, thinly sliced

1 Persian cucumber, diced

1 lime, cut into wedges

1. Place the noodles in a large bowl and completely cover with boiling water. Let stand for 3 to 5 minutes, until soft but still firm. Drain and set aside.

2. Line a plate with paper towel. In a large saucepan over medium-high heat, heat 1 tablespoon of the olive oil until shimmering. Add half the shrimp in a single layer and cook for 1 to 2 minutes, flipping once, until just pink. Using tongs, transfer the shrimp to the paper towel–lined plate. Repeat with the remaining shrimp.

3. Add the remaining 2 tablespoons olive oil to the pan and heat over medium-high heat until shimmering. Add the mushrooms and cook until golden, 4 to 5 minutes. Add the carrots, garlic, and ginger and cook, stirring, for an additional 4 minutes. Stir in the broth, soy sauce, 2½ cups water, ½ teaspoon salt, and ⅛ teaspoon pepper and bring to a boil.

4. Reduce the heat to maintain a simmer, stir in the kale, rice vinegar, sesame oil, chile pepper, and the noodles, and cook for 5 minutes. Return the shrimp to the pan, add the scallions, and cook for an additional 5 minutes.

5. Ladle the soup into four individual bowls, garnish with the cucumber, and serve with the lime wedges.

Continued

From the Market

Shrimp, large
(¾ pound, 15/20 count)

Rice vermicelli noodles
(4 ounces)

Baby kale (7 ounces)

Carrot (1 medium)

Persian cucumber (1)

Shiitake mushrooms (5 ounces)

Fresh red hot chile pepper (1)

Fresh ginger (1 large knob)

Scallions (1 bunch)

Garlic (4 cloves)

Lime (1)

From the Pantry

Extra-virgin olive oil
(3 tablespoons)

Low-sodium vegetable broth
(1 quart)

Low-sodium soy sauce
(3 tablespoons)

Kosher salt

Black pepper

Rice vinegar
(2 teaspoons)

Toasted sesame oil
(2 teaspoons)

Gluten-free: use tamari in place of soy sauce.

CHAPTER 8

Meat Mains

Spicy Chicken Tostadas
with Avocado Crema

4 TO 6 SERVINGS   TIME: 45 MINUTES

One of the things we love most about Mexican dinners is that you never leave the table hungry, and these tostadas are no exception. The tender chicken is the perfect foil for the crispy corn tortilla, and the luscious avocado crema adds a great balance to both.

FOR THE AVOCADO CREMA

1 ripe avocado, halved, pitted and peeled

¼ cup sour cream

1 tablespoon chopped fresh cilantro

2 tablespoons fresh lime juice

⅛ teaspoon sea salt

FOR THE CHICKEN TOSTADAS

3 large boneless, skinless chicken breasts
(about 1¾ pounds)

2 cups low-sodium chicken broth

2 tablespoons extra-virgin olive oil

1 cup chopped yellow onion

1 clove garlic, minced

½ cup tomato puree

1 canned chipotle chile pepper in adobo sauce,
finely chopped, plus 1 tablespoon sauce from the can

Sea salt

One 15-ounce can refried beans

4 cups vegetable oil, for frying, or as needed

8 corn tortillas

½ cup shredded iceberg lettuce

½ cup shredded red cabbage

½ cup grated carrots

1 cup shredded Monterey Jack cheese

1 lime, cut into wedges

FOR THE AVOCADO CREMA:

1. Combine all the crema ingredients in a food processor and process until smooth. Refrigerate until ready to use.

FOR THE CHICKEN TOSTADAS:

2. Place the chicken breasts in a large skillet. Add the broth and 2 cups water, cover the pan, and bring to a boil. Reduce the heat to medium and simmer, partially covered, for 20 minutes, or until the chicken is mostly cooked through. (The chicken will continue to cook with the onion.) Remove the chicken and the cooking liquid from the pan, reserving ½ cup of the liquid in a small bowl, and set the chicken aside just until cool enough to handle. Shred the chicken with a fork or your hands and set aside.

3. Wipe the skillet clean, return it to medium heat, and add 1 tablespoon of the olive oil. When the oil is shimmering, add the onion and cook until soft, about 5 minutes. Add the garlic and cook for an additional 2 minutes. Add the chicken and reserved cooking liquid, the tomato puree, chipotle pepper, adobo sauce, and ½ teaspoon salt and raise the heat to medium-high. Cook, stirring frequently, until the sauce has absorbed, about 5 minutes. Remove from the heat.

4. In a medium nonstick skillet, heat the remaining 1 tablespoon olive oil over medium-

Continued

high heat until shimmering. Add the refried beans. Cook, stirring occasionally, until the beans are soft and completely heated through, about 5 minutes. Set aside.

5. Line a baking sheet or large plate with paper towel and set it nearby. Fill a large skillet with the vegetable oil to a depth of ¾ to 1 inch (use more or less as needed) and heat over medium-high heat. (To determine if the oil is hot enough, insert the handle of a wooden spoon. If bubbles form around the wood and begin to float, the oil is ready.) Add a tortilla to the skillet and fry for 1 to 1½ minutes.

Using tongs, flip the tortilla and fry until crisp, an additional 1 to 1½ minutes. Remove the tortilla from the oil and place on the paper towel–lined baking sheet to drain. Season lightly with salt. Repeat with the remaining tortillas.

6. To assemble the tostadas, spread a layer of the beans on each tortilla. Spoon on a mound of the shredded chicken mixture, sprinkle with lettuce, cabbage, and carrots, add the shredded cheese, and finish with a generous dollop of the avocado crema on top. Serve with the lime wedges.

From the Market

Chicken breasts
(3 boneless, skinless,
about 1¾ pounds)

Avocado, ripe (1)

Iceberg lettuce (1 small head)

Red cabbage (1 small head)

Carrot (1 medium)

Yellow onion (1)

Garlic (1 clove)

Fresh cilantro (1 small bunch)

Limes (2)

Monterey Jack cheese (4 ounces)

Sour cream (¼ cup)

Tomato puree (½ cup)

Chipotle peppers in adobo sauce
(1 small can)

Corn tortillas (8)

From the Pantry

Sea salt

Extra-virgin olive oil
(2 tablespoons)

Low-sodium chicken broth
(2 cups)

Vegetable oil (1 quart)

Refried beans (one 15-ounce can)

Chicken Piccata
with Broccoli "Rice"

4 SERVINGS TIME: 40 MINUTES

We've steamed them, sautéed them, and roasted them, but "ricing" vegetables is a genius preparation when you're aiming to get more plants into your diet. It takes no time to turn broccoli or cauliflower into "rice," whether you use a food processor or a box grater. Tossed with a little oil and sautéed for just a few minutes, broccoli "rice" is a fabulous side to our buttery, lemony chicken piccata. It's an all-in-one classic Italian favorite, easy for a weeknight dinner yet elegant enough for company—this dish is a beauty.

FOR THE BROCCOLI "RICE"

1 large head broccoli (or 2 small),
cut into large florets with 2-inch stems

3 tablespoons extra-virgin olive oil

1 large clove garlic, minced

2 tablespoons unsalted butter

Kosher salt

Freshly ground black pepper

FOR THE CHICKEN

4 skinless, boneless chicken breast halves
(about 1¾ pounds), pounded to ¼ inch thick

Kosher salt

Freshly ground black pepper

½ cup all-purpose flour

4 tablespoons extra-virgin olive oil

¼ cup dry white wine

¾ cup low-sodium chicken broth

2 tablespoons fresh lemon juice

2 tablespoons capers, drained

2 tablespoons unsalted butter

1 tablespoon finely chopped fresh flat-leaf parsley

FOR THE BROCCOLI "RICE":

1. Place one-quarter of the broccoli florets in a food processor and pulse until broken down into pieces resembling rice. Transfer to a large bowl and repeat with the remaining broccoli. (Alternatively, grate the broccoli on the medium holes of a box grater.)

2. In a large skillet over medium-high heat, heat the olive oil until shimmering. Add the garlic and cook for 30 seconds. Add the broccoli rice and cook, stirring, for 3 to 4 minutes, until the broccoli begins to soften. Add the butter, 1 teaspoon salt, and ¼ teaspoon pepper. Cook until the butter has melted and the broccoli is tender, an additional 1 to 2 minutes. Transfer the broccoli rice to a serving platter that will be large enough to hold the chicken and tent with aluminum foil to keep warm. Wipe the skillet clean with a damp paper towel.

FOR THE CHICKEN:

3. Season the chicken with salt and pepper. Place the flour in a wide shallow dish and dredge each of the cutlets one at a time, shaking off any excess. Place them on a platter or baking sheet.

4. In the skillet you used for the broccoli rice, heat 2 tablespoons of the olive oil over medium-

Continued

high heat until shimmering. Add 2 of the cutlets and cook until golden brown, 2 to 2½ minutes. Flip the cutlets and cook until golden brown, an additional 2 to 2½ minutes. Transfer the cooked chicken to a large plate and tent with aluminum foil to keep warm. Repeat with the remaining 2 tablespoons olive oil to cook the remaining chicken and transfer to the tented plate. Discard any remaining oil in the skillet.

5. Return the skillet to medium-high heat. Add the wine and scrape the bottom with a wooden spoon for about 30 seconds to deglaze the pan. Add the broth, raise the heat to high, and bring to a boil. Cook for 3 to 4 minutes, until the liquid has reduced by half. Reduce the heat to medium and add the lemon juice and capers. Add ½ teaspoon salt and ⅛ teaspoon pepper. Return the chicken with any juices that have collected on the plate to the skillet and, using tongs or a spatula, flip them once, fully immersing them in the sauce. Reduce the heat to low.

6. Transfer the chicken to the serving platter, placing it over the broccoli rice.

7. Add the butter to the sauce in the pan and stir until the butter has melted and the sauce is bubbling. Pour the sauce over the chicken and broccoli rice and garnish with the parsley. Serve hot.

From the Market

Chicken breast halves
(4 small, 1¾ pounds total)

Broccoli
(1 large head or 2 small)

Garlic (1 large clove)

Fresh flat-leaf parsley
(1 small bunch)

Lemon (1)

Unsalted butter (4 tablespoons)

From the Pantry

Extra-virgin olive oil
(7 tablespoons)

Kosher salt

Black pepper

All-purpose flour
(½ cup)

Dry white wine
(¼ cup)

Low-sodium chicken broth
(¾ cup)

Capers (2 tablespoons)

Ratatouille Gratin with Chicken or Vegetarian Sausage

6 TO 8 SERVINGS   TIME: 1 HOUR 10 MINUTES

In the traditional Provençal ratatouille, the vegetables are prepared separately and then combined and cooked very slowly, resulting in a glorious and very flavorful vegetable stew. To save time, our method cooks the vegetables in pairs. We find that the end result is just as refined. Adding sausage and Gruyère cheese elevates a classic side dish to a complete meal.

3 small eggplant (1 pound), quartered lengthwise, then sliced crosswise into ½-inch-thick pieces

2 zucchini, halved lengthwise and cut into ½-inch-thick half-moons

1 yellow squash, halved lengthwise and cut into ½-inch-thick half-moons

Kosher salt

3 large heirloom or beefsteak tomatoes

5 tablespoons extra-virgin olive oil

2 chicken or vegetarian sausage links, cut into ½-inch-thick rounds

1 large Vidalia onion, sliced into ¼-inch-thick half-moons

1 red bell pepper, halved lengthwise and cut into ¼-inch-thick strips

1 yellow bell pepper, halved lengthwise and cut into ¼-inch-thick strips

2 cloves garlic, minced

Freshly ground black pepper

1 tablespoon tomato paste

1 tablespoon balsamic vinegar

2 tablespoons finely chopped fresh flat-leaf parsley

1 tablespoon chopped fresh thyme

1½ cups shredded Gruyère cheese

1. Place the eggplant, zucchini, and squash in a colander over a bowl and sprinkle with 2 teaspoons salt. Toss well and set aside for 30 minutes, then gently squeeze out any excess liquid with your hands.

2. Meanwhile, bring a large pot of water to a boil. Submerge the tomatoes in the boiling water, blanch for 10 seconds, and remove promptly. Set aside until cool enough to handle, then cut out the stems and peel the tomatoes. Cut each tomato in half crosswise, remove the seeds and juice, slice the tomatoes into ¼-inch-wide strips, and set aside.

3. Preheat the oven 375°F.

4. In a large cast-iron or other ovenproof skillet over medium-high heat, heat 1 tablespoon of the olive oil until shimmering. Add the sausage in one layer. Cook undisturbed until browned, 2 to 3 minutes. Flip and cook until browned, an additional 2 to 3 minutes. Transfer to a dish and set aside.

5. Add 1 tablespoon of the olive oil to the pan and heat over medium-high heat until shimmering. Add the onion and bell peppers. Sauté until tender, 5 to 7 minutes, then add the garlic, ¼ teaspoon salt, and ⅛ teaspoon black pepper. Sauté for an additional minute, then transfer the vegetables to a bowl and set aside.

6. Add the remaining 3 tablespoons olive oil to the skillet and heat over medium-high heat until shimmering. Add the eggplant, zucchini, and squash. Cook, stirring frequently, until tender, about 7 minutes. Return the onion and peppers to the skillet and stir to incorporate. Add the tomatoes, tomato paste, vinegar, parsley, thyme, ½ teaspoon salt, and ⅛ teaspoon black pepper and mix well. Return the sausage to the skillet and mix well. Place the skillet in the oven and bake for 10 minutes.

7. Remove the ratatouille from the oven, sprinkle it with the cheese, and bake for an additional 10 to 12 minutes, until the cheese is bubbling and browned. Serve hot.

From the Market

Sausage, chicken or vegetarian
(2 large links)

Eggplant (3 small, about 1 pound)

Zucchini (2 medium)

Yellow squash (1 medium)

Heirloom or beefsteak tomatoes
(3 large)

Red bell pepper (1 large)

Yellow bell pepper (1 large)

Vidalia onion (1 large)

Garlic (2 cloves)

Fresh flat-leaf parsley
(1 small bunch)

Fresh thyme (1 small bunch)

Gruyère cheese (6 ounces)

From the Pantry

Kosher salt

Extra-virgin olive oil (5 tablespoons)

Black pepper

Tomato paste
(1 tablespoon)

Balsamic vinegar (1 tablespoon)

Vegetarian: use vegetarian sausage.
Gluten-free: use gluten-free sausage.

Tandoori Chicken and Vegetable Sheet Pan Supper

4 SERVINGS   TIME: 1 HOUR PLUS 30 MINUTES MARINATING

Tandoori chicken gets its name from the vessel in which it's cooked: the tandoor, a traditional clay oven used to cook foods at a very high heat. Although we don't have a tandoor, we have devised a method to prepare this Indian dish at home. The longer you marinate the chicken and potatoes, the more intense the flavor. But we have found that even after only 30 minutes of marinating, the dish is infused with exotic, spicy flavors.

5 tablespoons organic canola oil

4 cloves garlic, minced

2 tablespoons grated fresh ginger

1 tablespoon chili powder

1 tablespoon garam masala

2 teaspoons ground cumin

2 teaspoons paprika

1 teaspoon ground turmeric

1 cup plain whole-milk yogurt

2 tablespoons fresh lime juice

1 jalapeño pepper, seeded and finely chopped

Kosher salt

Freshly ground black pepper

2 pounds bone-in, skin-on chicken parts
(a mix of breasts, split and cut in half, thighs, and legs)

¾ pound Yukon Gold potatoes, cut into 1-inch pieces

4 cups 1-inch cauliflower florets

4 cups 1-inch broccoli florets

8 small cremini mushrooms, stems trimmed

½ teaspoon fenugreek seeds or cumin seeds

½ cup red onion, halved lengthwise,
then sliced into thin half-moons

Mango Chutney (page 226) or your favorite
store-bought chutney (optional)

1. In a small skillet over medium heat, heat 2 tablespoons of the canola oil. Add the garlic and ginger and cook, stirring continuously, until light brown and fragrant, about 1 minute. Add the chili powder, garam masala, 1 teaspoon of the cumin, the paprika, and turmeric and cook, stirring continuously, for an additional minute. Set aside to cool.

2. In a large bowl, combine the yogurt, lime juice, jalapeño pepper, 2 teaspoons salt, ⅛ teaspoon black pepper, and the spice mixture and stir to combine.

3. Using a sharp knife, score the skin of each piece of chicken, making two or three shallow cuts about 1 inch apart. Add the chicken and potatoes to the bowl with the spiced yogurt and massage the yogurt into the chicken until all the pieces are well coated. Transfer the chicken, potatoes, and spiced yogurt to a large zip-top freezer bag and set aside for 30 minutes at room temperature or refrigerate for up to 8 hours.

4. Set a rack in the upper-third of the oven and preheat the oven to 425°F.

5. Place the cauliflower, broccoli, and mushrooms in a large bowl. Add the remaining 3 tablespoons canola oil, remaining 1 teaspoon cumin, the fenugreek seeds, ½ teaspoon salt, and ⅛ teaspoon black pepper and mix well.

6. Remove the marinated chicken from the bag, letting any excess marinade drip off, and arrange the pieces skin-side up on a rimmed baking sheet. Scatter the potatoes in and around the chicken. Roast for 20 minutes, then remove the pan from the oven and place the vegetables in a single layer in any spaces around the chicken. Return the pan

to the oven and roast for an additional 20 minutes. Remove from the oven and switch the oven to broil.

7. Sprinkle the red onion over the chicken and vegetables, return the baking sheet to the oven, and broil until the chicken is lightly charred and crispy, 2 to 3 minutes. Remove from the oven and serve with mango chutney, if desired.

From the Market

Chicken, mixed thighs, legs, and breasts (2 pounds bone-in, skin-on)

Cauliflower (1 head)

Broccoli (1 head)

Cremini (baby bella) mushrooms (8 small)

Yukon Gold potatoes (¾ pound)

Jalapeño pepper (1)

Fresh ginger (1 small knob)

Red onion (1 small)

Garlic (4 cloves)

Lime (1)

Yogurt, plain whole-milk (1 cup)

Garam masala (1 tablespoon)

Fenugreek seeds or cumin seeds (½ teaspoon)

Mango Chutney (page 226, or your favorite store-bought chutney; optional)

From the Pantry

Organic canola oil (5 tablespoons)

Chili powder (1 tablespoon)

Ground cumin (2 teaspoons)

Paprika (2 teaspoons)

Ground turmeric (1 teaspoon)

Kosher salt

Black pepper

Balsamic Chicken
with Caramelized Fennel

4 TO 6 SERVINGS   TIME: 1 HOUR

There was a little Italian restaurant in our neighborhood that had been a family favorite for more than twenty years. Everything they served was delicious, but the standout was the *pollo balsamico*. We have developed our own version with caramelized fennel, sage, and rosemary—a winning combination.

½ cup all-purpose flour

Kosher salt

Freshly ground black pepper

2 pounds boneless, skinless chicken breasts and thighs, cut into 2-inch chunks

2 large fennel bulbs

4 tablespoons extra-virgin olive oil

2 cloves garlic, lightly crushed

3 tablespoons unsalted butter

4 large shallots, cut into quarters

1 tablespoon roughly chopped fresh sage leaves

1 teaspoon roughly chopped fresh rosemary

½ cup red wine

½ cup low-sodium chicken broth

¼ cup good-quality balsamic vinegar

1. Place the flour in a wide shallow dish and season with ½ teaspoon salt and ⅛ teaspoon pepper. Dredge the chicken pieces in the flour and shake off the excess. Set the chicken pieces on a rimmed baking sheet or large plate. Set aside.

2. Cut the bottoms and the tops from the fennel bulbs and remove the outer layers, reserving some of the fronds for garnish. Slice the bulbs in half lengthwise, core them, and cut into thin slices, about ¼ inch thick. Set aside.

3. In a large skillet over medium-high heat, heat 2 tablespoons of the olive oil until shimmering. Add the garlic cloves and half the chicken pieces and cook until the chicken has formed a fine golden crust, about 4 minutes. Transfer the garlic to a platter. Flip the chicken pieces and cook, turning occasionally, until browned, an additional 3 to 4 minutes. Transfer the chicken to the platter. Add 1 tablespoon of the olive oil to the skillet, heat over medium-high heat until shimmering, and repeat to cook the remaining chicken. Set aside.

4. Add the remaining 1 tablespoon olive oil and 1 tablespoon of the butter to the skillet and heat over medium-high heat until shimmering. Add the fennel slices and cook, stirring, for 3 minutes. Reduce the heat to medium and add the shallot, sage, and rosemary. Cook, stirring frequently, until the vegetables are soft and golden brown,

about 9 minutes. Transfer the fennel-shallot mixture to the platter with the chicken and set aside.

5. Add the wine, broth, and remaining 2 tablespoons butter to the skillet, raise the heat to medium-high, and bring to a low boil. When the butter has melted, return the chicken and the fennel-shallot mixture to the pan and season with ½ teaspoon salt and ⅛ teaspoon pepper. Cook until the chicken is incorporated into the sauce, about 1 minute. Add the vinegar and cook, stirring frequently, until the sauce has thickened, 2 to 3 minutes. Transfer the chicken and vegetables to a serving platter, garnish with the reserved fennel fronds, and serve.

From the Market

Chicken, breasts and thighs (2 pounds boneless, skinless)

Fennel (2 large bulbs)

Shallots (4 large)

Garlic (2 cloves)

Fresh rosemary (a few sprigs)

Fresh sage (1 small bunch)

Unsalted butter (3 tablespoons)

From the Pantry

All-purpose flour (½ cup)

Kosher salt

Black pepper

Extra-virgin olive oil (¼ cup)

Red wine (½ cup)

Low-sodium chicken broth (½ cup)

Balsamic vinegar (¼ cup)

Dairy-free: use olive oil in place of butter

Skillet-Roasted Spatchcocked Chicken with Harvest Vegetables

4 SERVINGS   TIME: 1 HOUR 35 MINUTES PLUS OVERNIGHT

Judith Belzer and Michael Pollan know that crispy skin and juicy meat are the goals for a perfectly roasted chicken. So we turn to their amazing recipe, where they spatchcock—that is, butterfly—their bird, which exposes the whole chicken to the high temperatures in the oven, resulting in crispier skin. Since the breast and the legs are done at the same time, this method also produces moister meat. Best of all, the chicken is done in half the time. They've also upped the dish's health quotient by adding a cornucopia of harvest vegetables, turning it into an awesome one-skillet meal.

1 whole chicken (3½ to 4 pounds), backbone removed

Kosher salt

Freshly ground black pepper

⅓ cup plus 1 tablespoon extra-virgin olive oil

1 pound small Yukon Gold, red, or fingerling potatoes (or a mix), cut into ¾-inch pieces

10 ounces Brussels sprouts, cut in half

10 ounces cauliflower, cut into 1½-inch florets

3 medium carrots, cut into ¾-inch-thick pieces

2 medium red onions, cut into wedges

1 large turnip (about 12 ounces), peeled and cut into ¾-inch pieces

8 cloves garlic, whole

6 sprigs fresh rosemary

1. Season both sides of the chicken liberally with salt and pepper and refrigerate, uncovered, for at least 6 hours or preferably overnight.

2. Remove the chicken from the refrigerator 1 hour before cooking to allow it to come to room temperature.

3. Set a rack in the middle of the oven and preheat the oven to 400°F.

4. In a 14-inch or larger cast-iron or other ovenproof skillet over medium heat, heat the 1 tablespoon of olive oil until shimmering. Add the chicken, skin-side down. Cook undisturbed for 10 to 12 minutes, until a dark golden crust forms. Transfer the chicken to a platter. Set the skillet aside.

5. Meanwhile, in a large bowl, combine the potatoes, Brussels sprouts, cauliflower, carrots, onion, turnip, garlic, 3 rosemary sprigs, the remaining ⅓ cup olive oil, 1½ teaspoons salt, and ¼ teaspoon pepper. Toss well to coat. Add the vegetables to the skillet, lay the chicken skin-side up on top of the vegetables, and arrange the remaining 3 rosemary sprigs on top.

6. Roast the chicken and vegetables for 40 to 45 minutes, until the internal temperature of the chicken registers 165°F on an instant-read thermometer. Remove the skillet from the oven, transfer the chicken to a rimmed baking sheet or platter, and tent with aluminum foil. Turn and mix the vegetables with a wooden spoon. Return the skillet to the oven and roast the vegetables until browned, an additional 20 to 25 minutes.

7. When the vegetables are ready, carve the chicken. Separate the thighs and legs and cut the breasts in half. Place the vegetables in the middle of a serving platter, arrange the chicken pieces around the sides, and serve hot.

From the Market

Whole chicken (3½ to 4 pounds), backbone removed (you can ask your butcher to remove it)

Small Yukon Gold, red, or fingerling potatoes, or a mix (1 pound)

Brussels sprouts (10 ounces)

Cauliflower (1 small head)

Carrots (3 medium)

Turnip (1 large, about 12 ounces)

Red onions (2 medium)

Garlic (8 cloves)

Fresh rosemary (6 sprigs)

From the Pantry

Kosher salt

Black pepper

Extra-virgin olive oil (⅓ cup plus 1 tablespoon)

Sheet Pan Turkish-Spiced Chicken

4 TO 6 SERVINGS   TIME: 1 HOUR PLUS 1 HOUR MARINATING

We've lavished our sheet pan–roasted chicken with an array of zesty, fragrant Turkish spices—your kitchen will smell incredible as this dinner cooks in the oven. As with any sheet pan dish, be careful to leave space between the ingredients so the chicken, sweet potatoes, and onions can caramelize and brown, getting crispy around the edges instead of steaming. We finish the dish by piling on a cool salad that offers a sharp contrast to the vibrant, spicy chicken.

FOR THE MARINADE

½ cup extra-virgin olive oil

3 tablespoons fresh lemon juice

2 teaspoons ground cumin

2 teaspoons ground coriander

2 teaspoons paprika

1 teaspoon smoked paprika

1 teaspoon ground turmeric

½ teaspoon ground cinnamon

¼ teaspoon cayenne pepper

¼ teaspoon crushed red pepper flakes, or to taste

6 cloves garlic, minced

1 teaspoon kosher salt

½ teaspoon freshly ground black pepper

FOR THE CHICKEN

6 bone-in, skin-on chicken thighs

Organic olive oil cooking spray

2 medium yellow onions, quartered

2 small sweet potatoes, peeled and cut into ¾-inch-thick rounds

Kosher salt

Freshly ground black pepper

2 tomatoes, quartered

¾ cup quartered cucumber rounds

½ cup pitted green or black olives

⅓ cup roughly chopped fresh flat-leaf parsley

FOR THE MARINADE:

1. In a small bowl, whisk together all the marinade ingredients until well combined.

FOR THE CHICKEN:

2. Place the chicken in a large zip-top plastic bag. Pour in the marinade, seal, and turn to completely coat. Let it marinate at room temperature for 1 hour or refrigerate for up to overnight. Remove the chicken from the refrigerator 1 hour before cooking to let it come to room temperature.

3. Set the oven racks in the middle and upper thirds of the oven and preheat the oven to 425°F. Spray a rimmed baking sheet with cooking spray.

4. Remove the chicken from the marinade and place it skin-side up on the baking sheet. Arrange the onion and sweet potatoes in a single layer around the chicken, cover all with the marinade, and turn once to coat. Season lightly with salt and pepper. Roast on the middle rack until the chicken is browned and the vegetables are tender, 35 to 45 minutes. Remove the baking sheet from the oven and switch the oven to broil. When the broiler is heated, return the pan to the upper rack of the oven and broil until the skin is crisp, 5 to 8 minutes.

5. Remove from the oven and arrange the chicken and vegetables on a serving platter. Scatter the tomatoes, cucumbers, olives, and parsley on top. Season with salt and pepper and serve.

Continued

Food for Thought

Herbs and spices do so much more than simply improve the flavors of dishes—they also provide impressive health benefits. In fact, many spices are antioxidant powerhouses—equal to full servings of many fruits and vegetables. For example, ½ teaspoon of cloves contains more antioxidants than ½ cup of blueberries. Studies indicate that dried herbs are at least as beneficial as their fresh counterparts. Particularly healthful herbs and spices include cloves, oregano, turmeric, cinnamon, and dried red chile pepper.

From the Market

Chicken thighs (6 bone-in, skin-on, about 2½ pounds)

Cucumber (1 medium)

Tomatoes (2)

Sweet potatoes (2 small)

Yellow onions (2 medium)

Garlic (6 cloves)

Fresh flat-leaf parsley (1 bunch)

Lemons (2)

Black or green olives, pitted (½ cup)

From the Pantry

Extra-virgin olive oil (½ cup)

Ground cumin (2 teaspoons)

Ground coriander (2 teaspoons)

Paprika (2 teaspoons)

Smoked paprika (1 teaspoon)

Ground turmeric (1 teaspoon)

Ground cinnamon (½ teaspoon)

Cayenne pepper (¼ teaspoon)

Crushed red pepper flakes (¼ teaspoon)

Kosher salt

Black pepper

Organic olive oil cooking spray

Kale Pesto–Glazed Chicken Breasts

4 SERVINGS   TIME: 45 MINUTES

We enjoy a classic basil pesto, but have discovered that you can make delectable pesto from almost any fresh herb. It's fun creating new variations by switching up the greens, nuts, or oils used. We soon realized that kale could double as the "herb" in a pesto *and* the vegetable on our plate. This meal comes together very quickly, making it ideal for a weeknight.

FOR THE KALE PESTO

⅓ cup raw walnuts

3 cups tightly packed baby kale

3 cloves garlic, halved

½ cup freshly grated Parmesan cheese

Sea salt

Freshly ground black pepper

½ cup extra-virgin olive oil

FOR THE CHICKEN

¼ cup extra-virgin olive oil

1 tablespoon minced garlic

⅓ cup dry vermouth

1 tablespoon lemon zest

1 tablespoon fresh lemon juice

Kosher salt

Freshly ground black pepper

4 boneless, skin-on chicken breasts
(6 to 8 ounces each)

4 tablespoons freshly grated Parmesan cheese

1 lemon, cut into 8 wedges

FOR THE KALE PESTO:

1. In a dry skillet over medium-high heat, toast the walnuts, shaking the pan and stirring until they begin to brown, 3 to 5 minutes. Transfer to a plate and let cool.

2. In a food processor or blender, pulse the kale in batches until roughly chopped. Add the cooled walnuts and garlic and pulse to combine. Scrape down the sides with a rubber spatula and add the Parmesan cheese, ½ teaspoon salt, and ⅛ teaspoon pepper. Pulse until smooth. With the motor running, slowly drizzle in the olive oil and pulse to combine. Set aside.

FOR THE CHICKEN:

3. Set a rack in the upper third of the oven and preheat the oven to 400°F.

4. In a small saucepan over medium-low heat, heat the olive oil. Add the garlic and cook for 1½ minutes. Remove from the heat and stir in the vermouth, lemon zest, lemon juice, ½ teaspoon salt, and ⅛ teaspoon pepper. Pour the sauce into a 9 by 13-inch casserole or baking dish.

5. Blot any excess moisture from the chicken breasts and season them liberally with salt and pepper. Place the chicken skin-side up in the sauce. Cover each chicken breast with 1 tablespoon of the pesto, spreading it evenly. Bake the chicken for 30 to 40 minutes, until the

Continued

internal temperature registers 165°F on an instant-read thermometer. Remove from the oven and switch the oven to broil.

6. Sprinkle each breast with 1 tablespoon of the Parmesan cheese. Broil for 2 minutes, or until the pesto is bubbling and the cheese has melted. Serve the chicken with the pan juices drizzled over the top and garnished with the lemon wedges.

TO STORE THE REMAINING PESTO FOR LATER USE, TRANSFER IT TO AN AIRTIGHT CONTAINER AND TOP WITH 2 TO 3 TABLESPOONS EXTRA-VIRGIN OLIVE OIL. STORE IN THE REFRIGERATOR FOR 7 TO 10 DAYS OR IN THE FREEZER FOR UP TO 6 MONTHS.

From the Market
Chicken breasts (4 boneless, skin-on, 6 to 8 ounces each)
Baby kale (10 ounces)
Garlic (6 cloves)
Lemons (2)

Parmesan cheese (3 ounces)

From the Pantry
Raw walnuts (⅓ cup)
Sea salt

Black pepper
Kosher salt
Extra-virgin olive oil (¾ cup)
Dry vermouth (⅓ cup)

Chicken Scarpariello with Escarole

4 TO 6 SERVINGS   TIME: 45 MINUTES

Spicy and sweet, much of the pleasure of this dish is the pan sauce. White wine, pickled peppers, chicken broth, and loads of garlic create a truly delectable savory sauce. The Italian green escarole blends beautifully with the crispy chicken bites.

6 bone-in, skin-on chicken thighs

Kosher salt

Freshly ground black pepper

2 tablespoons extra-virgin olive oil

2 sweet Italian sausages (about 6 ounces)

1 hot Italian sausage (about 3 ounces)

1 large Spanish onion, halved lengthwise and thinly sliced into half-moons

1 red bell pepper, thinly sliced

6 cloves garlic, thinly sliced

2 sprigs fresh rosemary

10 sweet pickled Peppadew peppers in brine, drained

1 pound escarole, cleaned, cored, and cut into ½-inch-wide ribbons

1 cup dry white wine

1 cup low-sodium chicken broth

1 tablespoon chopped fresh flat-leaf parsley

1. Set a rack in the middle of the oven and preheat the oven to 450°F.

2. Season the chicken liberally with salt and black pepper.

3. In a large Dutch oven over medium-high heat, heat the olive oil until shimmering. Add the chicken, skin-side down, and cook undisturbed until the skin is golden, 8 to 10 minutes. Flip the chicken and cook until browned, about 3 minutes more. Transfer the chicken to a large platter and set aside. (The chicken will not be fully cooked but will finish cooking in the oven.)

4. Add the sausages to the pot and cook over medium heat, turning occasionally, until browned on all sides, about 6 minutes. Transfer the sausages to a cutting board, let cool slightly, and cut into ½-inch-thick rounds. Set aside. (The sausage will not be fully cooked but will finish cooking in the oven.)

5. Add the onion, bell pepper, and garlic to the pot and cook, stirring with a wooden spoon, for 3 to 4 minutes, until softened and lightly browned. Add the rosemary and Peppadew peppers and stir, scraping up the browned bits from the sides and bottom of the pot. Add the escarole, 1 teaspoon salt, and ⅛ teaspoon black pepper and cook, stirring, for 2 minutes. Stir in the wine and broth and cook for an additional

Continued

minute. Return the sausages to the pot and stir to combine. Return the chicken to the pot, nestling it among the vegetables. Cover, transfer the pot to the oven, and cook until the internal temperature of the chicken registers 165°F on an instant-read thermometer, 15 to 20 minutes.

6. Discard the rosemary sprigs, garnish with the parsley, and serve hot.

From the Market

Chicken thighs
(6 bone-in, skin-on)

Italian sausages
(2 sweet, 1 hot; about
3 ounces each)

Red bell pepper (1)

Escarole (1 pound)

Spanish onion (1 large)

Garlic (6 cloves)

Fresh rosemary (1 bunch)

Fresh flat-leaf parsley (1 bunch)

Sweet pickled Peppadew peppers (10)

From the Pantry

Kosher salt

Black pepper

Extra-virgin olive oil
(2 tablespoons)

Dry white wine (1 cup)

Low-sodium chicken broth
(1 cup)

Dry-Fried Beef with Vegetables

4 SERVINGS TIME: 35 MINUTES

Dry-frying removes moisture from meat, thereby concentrating its flavor. The beef in this stir-fry becomes caramelized and, combined with the fiery chile peppers, achieves a harmonious balance of sweet and spicy in each bite. For our recipe, we have reduced the amount of beef commonly used and upped the vegetable quotient by adding zucchini, carrots, and celery. We love to serve this dish over a bowl of rice, noodles, or our Rice Noodle Nests (page 220).

1 pound flank steak

3 teaspoons low-sodium soy sauce

3 teaspoons rice vinegar

2 tablespoons fermented bean paste

1 tablespoon dry sherry

2 teaspoons sugar

½ cup organic canola oil

3 carrots, julienned

3 celery stalks, julienned

1 clove garlic, minced

2 teaspoons minced fresh ginger

1 medium zucchini, julienned

2 scallions, white and light green parts only, thinly sliced

2 dried red chile peppers

2 teaspoons ground toasted Sichuan peppercorns

1. Cut the steak along the grain into 3-inch strips. Cut each strip across the grain into ¼-inch strips and set aside.

2. In a medium bowl (large enough to hold all the steak), combine 1 teaspoon of the soy sauce and 1 teaspoon of the vinegar.

3. In a small bowl, combine the remaining 2 teaspoons soy sauce, remaining 2 teaspoons vinegar, the bean paste, sherry, and sugar. Stir until the sugar has dissolved, 1 to 2 minutes. Set aside.

4. Line a rimmed baking sheet or plate with paper towel and set it nearby.

5. Place the steak and the canola oil in a wok and cook over medium-high heat, stirring occasionally. The steak will release its moisture and then begin to fry. Cook until the steak is nicely browned, 9 to 10 minutes. Remove from the oil with a slotted spoon and transfer to the paper towel–lined baking sheet to drain.

6. Add the beef to the bowl with the soy sauce–vinegar mixture and toss to combine.

7. Remove all but 1 tablespoon of the oil from the wok and heat the oil over high heat until it begins to smoke. Add the carrots and celery and cook, stirring, for 30 seconds. Add the garlic, ginger, zucchini, scallions, and chile peppers and stir for an additional 30 seconds. Stir in the steak, soy sauce–vinegar mixture, and Sichuan peppercorns and toss until combined, about 30 seconds more. Serve hot.

From the Market

Flank steak (1 pound)

Carrots (3 medium)

Celery (3 stalks)

Zucchini (1 medium)

Fresh ginger (1 knob)

Scallions (2)

Garlic (1 clove)

Fermented bean paste
(2 tablespoons)

Dried red chile peppers (2 whole)

Sichuan peppercorns (2 teaspoons)

From the Pantry

Low-sodium soy sauce
(1 tablespoon)

Rice vinegar (1 tablespoon)

Dry sherry (1 tablespoon)

Granulated sugar (2 teaspoons)

Organic canola oil (½ cup)

Gluten-free: use tamari in place of
soy sauce. Use gluten-free fermented
bean paste.

CHAPTER 9

Sides

Smashed Potatoes with Shredded Brussels Sprouts

4 SERVINGS   TIME: 55 MINUTES

There is something synergistic about roasted potatoes and Brussels sprouts—their combined taste is even better than the individual elements. For this recipe we tried something a little different: We finely shredded the Brussels sprouts before adding them to the potatoes already roasting in the oven. The result—tender potatoes topped with crispy Brussels sprouts—is a delightfully flavorful side dish. And if you love potatoes but are trying to cut back a little on starch, this is a perfect way to do it.

3 tablespoons extra-virgin olive oil, plus extra for greasing

1¼ pounds small white or red potatoes, scrubbed but not peeled

Sea salt

2 cloves garlic, minced

½ teaspoon paprika

Freshly ground black pepper

2 cups tightly packed finely shredded Brussels sprouts

1 teaspoon lightly packed fresh thyme leaves

1. Preheat the oven to 425°F. Lightly grease a rimmed baking sheet with olive oil.

2. Place the potatoes in a large pot and add water to cover and 1 teaspoon salt. Cover the pot and bring the water to a boil. Reduce the heat to medium-high and cook, uncovered, until the potatoes are fork-tender, 15 to 20 minutes.

3. Meanwhile, in a small bowl, whisk together 2 tablespoons of the olive oil, the garlic, paprika, ½ teaspoon salt, and ¼ teaspoon pepper until well combined. Set aside.

4. In a medium bowl, combine the Brussels sprouts, the remaining 1 tablespoon olive oil, ½ teaspoon salt, and ¼ teaspoon pepper. Mix well and set aside.

5. Drain the potatoes in a colander. Place them on the prepared baking sheet, leaving space between them. Using a potato masher, fork, or the bottom of a glass, gently but firmly press down on each potato until somewhat flattened but whole. (Don't worry if they break apart slightly; simply push them back together with your fingers.)

6. Using a pastry brush, coat the top of each potato with the oil-garlic mixture and sprinkle each with a couple of thyme leaves. Roast until the potatoes begin to turn golden brown, 15 to 20 minutes. Remove the baking sheet from the oven and spread the Brussels sprouts on the sheet in the spaces between the potatoes. Rotate the sheet and roast until the Brussels sprouts are crisp and browned, about 10 minutes more. Transfer to a platter, season with additional salt and pepper, and serve hot.

From the Market

Small white or red potatoes (1¼ pounds)

Brussels sprouts (9 ounces)

Garlic (2 cloves)

Fresh thyme (2 sprigs)

From the Pantry

Sea salt

Extra-virgin olive oil (3 tablespoons)

Paprika (½ teaspoon)

Black pepper

Sautéed Baby Beets with Balsamic Beet Greens

4 TO 6 SERVINGS TIME: 20 MINUTES

When fresh beets are in season, this dish is a great way to showcase every part of the plant. In one bite, you get moist morsels of sautéed beet, as well as flavorful, garlicky beet greens seasoned with earthy balsamic vinegar—the two elements really complement each other beautifully.

2 bunches baby beets, with greens attached

2 tablespoons extra-virgin olive oil

Kosher salt

Freshly ground black pepper

1 teaspoon unsalted butter

2 cloves garlic, minced

⅛ teaspoon crushed red pepper flakes

1 teaspoon balsamic vinegar

1. Remove the beet greens and set aside. Trim and scrub the beets and cut them into ½-inch pieces. Stem the greens, rinse well, and cut the leaves into 2-inch pieces.

2. In a medium skillet over medium heat, heat 1 tablespoon of the olive oil until shimmering. Add the beets and cook, stirring occasionally, until tender, 10 to 12 minutes. Season lightly with salt and pepper.

3. Meanwhile, in a separate large skillet over medium heat, heat the remaining 1 tablespoon olive oil with the butter until the butter has melted. Add the garlic and red pepper flakes and sauté for 30 seconds. Add the beet greens and cook, stirring, until wilted, 3 to 5 minutes. Stir in the vinegar, ¼ teaspoon salt, and ⅛ teaspoon pepper.

4. Arrange the beet greens on a serving plate, top with the sautéed beets, season with additional salt and pepper, and serve hot.

Food for Thought

The beet plant is a nutritional powerhouse. Beets are particularly rich in nitrates, which have been shown to lower blood pressure, boost stamina, and fight inflammation. What's more, beets have been shown to have protective effects on the brain that could help prevent Alzheimer's disease. And don't toss the greens when you're preparing beets—they are the healthiest part of the plant, containing an abundance of vital nutrients, vitamins, and minerals. They are a particularly excellent vegetarian source of iron (more so than spinach), calcium, potassium, magnesium, and fiber.

From the Market
Baby beets, with greens attached (2 bunches)
Garlic (2 cloves)
Unsalted butter (1 teaspoon)

From the Pantry
Extra-virgin olive oil (2 tablespoons)
Crushed red pepper flakes (⅛ teaspoon)
Balsamic vinegar (1 teaspoon)

Kosher salt
Black pepper

Vegan/Dairy-free: use olive oil in place of butter.

Roasted Delicata Squash Rings with Crispy Sage

4 TO 6 SERVINGS TIME: 55 MINUTES

This is our new all-time favorite vegetable side. The sweet and velvety squash is so easy to make and pairs perfectly with almost any dinner, though we particularly like serving it with our Kale Pesto–Glazed Chicken Breasts (page 191) or Transcendent Burgers (page 100) in lieu of fries.

2 delicata squash (about 2 pounds), ends trimmed

20 to 25 fresh sage leaves

2 tablespoons extra-virgin olive oil

¼ teaspoon crushed red pepper flakes, or to taste

Kosher salt

Freshly ground black pepper

1. Set racks in the upper and lower thirds of the oven and preheat the oven to 425°F. Line two rimmed baking sheets with parchment paper.

2. Slice each squash in half crosswise and scoop out the seeds with a spoon. Slice the squash into ¼-inch-thick rings.

3. In a large bowl, combine the squash, sage leaves, olive oil, red pepper flakes, ¼ teaspoon salt, and ⅛ teaspoon black pepper. Mix well.

4. Arrange the squash rings and sage leaves on the baking sheets in a single layer. Roast until golden brown, 15 to 20 minutes.

5. Remove the baking sheets from the oven, flip the squash, and return the baking sheets to the oven, rotating the sheets top to bottom. Roast until the squash is golden brown, an additional 15 to 20 minutes. Transfer the squash and sage to a platter and serve hot.

From the Market
Delicata squash
(2, about 2 pounds)
Fresh sage (1 bunch)

From the Pantry
Extra-virgin olive oil
(2 tablespoons)
Kosher salt
Black pepper

Crushed red pepper flakes
(¼ teaspoon)

Charred Broccolini with Smoked Paprika and Pepitas

4 TO 6 SERVINGS   TIME: 30 MINUTES

Roasting Broccolini at a high temperature results in a rich flavor that pairs well with smoked paprika. The tender, caramelized Broccolini and the crunchy pepitas (pumpkin seeds) complement each other perfectly. This is an easy weeknight vegetable dish, but it also makes an elegant side for a party.

3 tablespoons extra-virgin olive oil

½ teaspoon smoked paprika

1½ pounds Broccolini, ends trimmed, any thick stalks halved lengthwise

Kosher salt

Freshly ground black pepper

2 tablespoons raw shelled pumpkin seeds (pepitas)

⅓ cup crumbled ricotta salata cheese

1. Preheat the oven to 425°F.

2. In a small saucepan over medium-low heat, heat the olive oil and paprika until warm and smoky, 2 to 3 minutes. Let cool slightly.

3. Place the Broccolini on a rimmed baking sheet, drizzle with the spiced oil, and toss. Spread the Broccolini over the baking sheet in a single layer, making sure to leave space between the stalks. Sprinkle with ¼ teaspoon salt and ⅛ teaspoon pepper. Roast for 10 minutes, then remove from the oven and flip the Broccolini. Sprinkle with the pumpkin seeds and cheese. Return them to the oven and roast until the Broccolini is nicely charred and the cheese has browned (it will not melt), 8 to 9 minutes.

4. Transfer to a platter and serve hot.

From the Market
Broccolini
(1½ pounds)
Ricotta salata cheese
(2 ounces)

From the Pantry
Extra-virgin olive oil
(3 tablespoons)
Smoked paprika
(½ teaspoon)

Kosher salt
Black pepper
Raw shelled pumpkin seeds
(pepitas) (2 tablespoons)

Thyme-Roasted Baby Rainbow Carrots

4 TO 6 SERVINGS   TIME: 35 MINUTES

The vibrant color of this simple side makes it a real stunner—and it tastes just as good as it looks. Our kids especially love this one; two of them, who happened to be home for a college break when we were testing the recipe, gobbled up these carrots before they even made it to the dinner table!

2 pounds baby rainbow carrots*
(if not available, use small carrots), trimmed

2 tablespoons extra-virgin olive oil

2 teaspoons minced fresh thyme

Sea salt

Freshly ground black pepper

1 tablespoon finely chopped fresh flat-leaf parsley

1. Set the racks in the upper and lower thirds of the oven and preheat the oven to 425°F.

2. In a large bowl, combine the carrots, olive oil, thyme, ½ teaspoon salt, and ¼ teaspoon pepper and mix thoroughly to coat.

3. Arrange the carrots in a single layer on two rimmed baking sheets, making sure not to crowd them. Cover the baking sheets with aluminum foil and roast for 10 minutes. Remove from the oven, take off the foil, and return the baking sheets to the oven, switching their positions between the upper and lower racks. Roast until the carrots are caramelized, an additional 10 to 12 minutes.

4. Sprinkle with the parsley, transfer to a platter, and serve hot.

Food for Thought

We all know that carrots are high in vitamin A, which means they're great for our eyes, but we didn't realize they're also good for our hearts. One study showed that participants who ate approximately 1 cup of carrots each day for three weeks had lowered blood cholesterol levels. Carrots are also rich in potassium, which helps lower blood pressure, increase blood flow, and aid circulation. In addition, they contain high levels of beta-carotene, vitamin C, and fiber. And no matter how you eat them—raw, cooked, or juiced—carrots maintain their health benefits.

From the Market

Baby rainbow carrots or small carrots* (2 pounds, about 3 bunches)

Fresh thyme (1 small bunch)

Fresh flat-leaf parsley (1 small bunch)

* Use young carrots, not packaged "baby" carrots.

From the Pantry

Extra-virgin olive oil (2 tablespoons)

Sea salt

Black pepper

Three Pepper Stir-Fried Cabbage

4 TO 6 SERVINGS TIME: 20 MINUTES

We love this stir-fry because it is so quick and simple to make and packs a lot of flavor. The three varieties of pepper add a fiery spice to the sweet-savoriness of the cabbage. We like to serve it as a side, but you could also pair it with a grain or cauliflower "rice" for a complete plant-based main.

2 tablespoons organic canola oil

1 teaspoon whole Sichuan peppercorns (if not available, use black peppercorns)

2 cloves garlic, minced

1 fresh medium-spicy red chile pepper (such as Thai bird or cayenne), sliced

1 tablespoon chopped seeded dried red chile pepper

1 teaspoon grated fresh ginger

1 small head white cabbage, quartered, cored, and sliced into bite-size strips

2 tablespoons low-sodium soy sauce

1 tablespoon rice vinegar

2 teaspoons toasted sesame oil

1 teaspoon granulated sugar

2 scallions, white and light green parts only, thinly sliced

Kosher salt

Heat a wok or large sauté pan over medium-high heat. When the wok is hot, add the canola oil and peppercorns. Stir until the peppercorns become fragrant and darken, about 1 minute, then remove with a slotted spoon and discard. Add the garlic, the fresh and dried chile peppers, and the ginger to the oil. Cook, stirring continuously, for 1 minute. Raise the heat to high, add the cabbage, and cook, stirring continuously, until it begins to wilt, 3 to 5 minutes. Add the soy sauce, vinegar, sesame oil, and sugar and stir to incorporate. Add the scallions and cook until the cabbage is beginning to brown in spots, 2 to 3 minutes. Season lightly with salt and serve hot.

Food for Thought

White cabbage aids in cancer prevention thanks to its antioxidant properties, and helps protect against cardiovascular disease as well as type 2 diabetes. It's also a terrific source of fiber and chock-full of vitamins K, C, and B6.

From the Market

White cabbage (1 small head)

Fresh red chile pepper, medium-spicy, such as Thai bird or cayenne (1)

Scallions (2)

Garlic (2 cloves)

Fresh ginger (1 small knob)

Sichuan peppercorns (1 teaspoon) or if not available, use black peppercorns

From the Pantry

Organic canola oil (2 tablespoons)

Dried red chile peppers (3)

Low-sodium soy sauce (2 tablespoons)

Rice vinegar (1 tablespoon)

Toasted sesame oil (2 teaspoons)

Granulated sugar (1 teaspoon)

Kosher salt

Vegan: use turbinado sugar in place of granulated. Gluten-free: use tamari in place of soy sauce.

Golden Roasted Quinoa

4 TO 6 SERVINGS TIME: 1 HOUR

In this recipe we first toast the quinoa and then roast it with aromatics to bring out its full flavor. Roasting gives it a delicate, nutty crunch, which will win over even quinoa skeptics. A complete protein source on its own, quinoa is the perfect base or side for any vegetarian or vegan dish and also pairs nicely with chicken, fish, and meat.

1½ cups uncooked quinoa

3 cups low-sodium vegetable broth

1 tablespoon extra-virgin olive oil

2 tablespoons finely chopped fresh flat-leaf parsley

2 cloves garlic, minced

Sea salt

Freshly ground black pepper

1. Preheat the oven to 400°F. Line a rimmed baking sheet with parchment paper.

2. In a dry medium saucepan over medium heat, toast the quinoa, stirring often, until lightly browned and fragrant, 3 to 5 minutes. Add the broth, raise the heat to high, and bring to a boil. Reduce the heat to low, cover, and simmer until the broth has been absorbed, 20 to 25 minutes.

3. Transfer the quinoa to a large bowl. Add the olive oil, parsley, garlic, ½ teaspoon salt, and ⅛ teaspoon pepper and mix well with a wooden spoon.

4. Spread the quinoa over the prepared baking sheet and roast until golden brown, 20 to 25 minutes, stirring halfway through. Season with additional salt and pepper and serve hot.

From the Market
Garlic (2 cloves)
Fresh flat-leaf parsley (1 small bunch)

From the Pantry
Quinoa (1½ cups)
Low-sodium vegetable broth (3 cups)
Extra-virgin olive oil (1 tablespoon)

Sea salt
Black pepper
*You will need parchment paper.

Wild Mushroom Sauté with Shaved Parmesan

4 TO 6 SERVINGS TIME: 15 MINUTES

The mushrooms in this sauté are cooked down with butter and shallots and become caramelized, tender, and scrumptious. This is a terrific side dish for any meal, as well as a perfect topping for burgers, grilled steaks, baked potatoes, creamy polenta, or cheesy grits.

3 tablespoons extra-virgin olive oil

2 tablespoons finely chopped shallot

1 tablespoon unsalted butter

3 cloves garlic, minced

1¾ pounds assorted fresh wild mushrooms, such as portobello, porcini, cremini, oyster, chanterelle, and morel (trimmed), shiitake (stems removed), and thickly sliced

Kosher salt

Freshly ground black pepper

2 tablespoons finely chopped fresh flat-leaf parsley

½ cup shaved Parmesan cheese

1. In a large heavy skillet over low heat, heat the olive oil until shimmering. Add the shallot and cook until translucent, about 2 minutes. Add the butter. When it has melted, stir in the garlic. Raise the heat to medium, add the mushrooms, 1 teaspoon salt, and ¼ teaspoon pepper, and mix well. Cook, stirring often, for 8 to 9 minutes, until the mushrooms are tender and have released their liquid. Turn off the heat and stir in the parsley. Season with salt and pepper.

2. Divide among individual plates and top each with the shaved Parmesan. Serve hot.

From the Market

Assorted fresh wild mushrooms, such as shiitake, portobello, porcini, cremini (baby bella), oyster, chanterelle, and morel (1¾ pounds)

Shallots (2 small)

Garlic (3 cloves)

Fresh flat-leaf parsley (1 small bunch)

Unsalted butter (1 tablespoon)

Parmesan cheese (2 ounces)

From the Pantry

Extra-virgin olive oil (3 tablespoons)

Kosher salt

Black pepper

Baked Accordion Potatoes
with Paprika and Thyme

4 TO 6 SERVINGS   TIME: 1 HOUR 5 MINUTES

This recipe for accordion potatoes is based on the famed Hasselback potato, a Swedish baked potato dish that got its name back in the 1940s from the Hasselbacken Hotel in Stockholm, where it was the hotel's signature dish. There are many versions of this dish, but we've simplified and "healthified" ours—we leave out the bread crumbs and cheese and add the savory seasonings paprika and thyme.

2 tablespoons extra-virgin olive oil, plus more for greasing

3 tablespoons unsalted butter, melted

1 teaspoon paprika

1 teaspoon minced fresh thyme leaves, plus 4 or 5 sprigs

Sea salt

Freshly ground black pepper

2 pounds 2- to 3-inch-long Yukon Gold potatoes, scrubbed but not peeled

1. Preheat the oven to 425°F. Grease a rimmed baking sheet or baking dish with olive oil.

2. In a small bowl, combine the melted butter, olive oil, paprika, minced thyme, ½ teaspoon salt, and ¼ teaspoon pepper and mix well.

3. Cut crosswise slits about ⅛ inch apart all along each potato, taking care not to slice all the way through—leave about ¼ inch intact at the bottom. (If you place the potato in a large wooden spoon while you cut, it is much easier not to cut too deeply.) Once cut, gently fan each potato open.

4. Place the potatoes cut-side up on the prepared baking sheet or dish. Using a pastry brush, coat them all over with half the butter mixture. Arrange the thyme sprigs on top.

5. Place in the preheated oven and bake for 30 minutes.

6. Remove the potatoes from the oven, fan them out a little more, and brush with the remaining butter mixture, letting it drip into the slits. Bake for an additional 25 to 30 minutes, until the edges are crisp. Season generously with additional salt and serve hot.

From the Market

Yukon Gold potatoes
(2 pounds; about 8,
each 2 to 3 inches long)

Fresh thyme (1 small bunch)

Unsalted butter
(3 tablespoons)

From the Pantry

Extra-virgin olive oil
(2 tablespoons, plus extra
for greasing)

Paprika (1 teaspoon)

Sea salt

Black pepper

Vegan/Dairy-free: use olive oil in place of butter.

Brown Butter Asparagus
with Melted Fontina and Pistachios

4 TO 6 SERVINGS TIME: 15 MINUTES

We barely get this one out of the oven before it is gobbled up. The combination of the nutty Fontina cheese, brown butter, and crunchy pistachios is irresistible. This dish is also visually stunning, so keep it in mind when you have friends over.

Kosher salt

2 pounds asparagus, trimmed

2 tablespoons unsalted butter

Freshly ground black pepper

4 ounces Italian Fontina cheese, thinly sliced

¼ cup unsalted shelled pistachios, roughly chopped

1. Preheat the oven to broil.

2. Fill a large ovenproof (preferably cast-iron) skillet with 1 inch of water and add ½ teaspoon salt. Bring the water to a boil, then add the asparagus in a single layer and cook for 3 to 4 minutes, until crisp-tender. Drain the asparagus.

3. In the same skillet over high heat, melt the butter and cook until foamy and lightly browned. Reduce the heat to low, return the cooked asparagus to the skillet, and gently shake the pan to coat it with the butter. Remove from the heat and season with salt and pepper.

4. Lay the slices of cheese on top of the asparagus and sprinkle with the pistachios. Broil until the cheese is melted and light golden brown, 1 to 3 minutes. Serve hot.

From the Market

Asparagus (2 pounds)

Unsalted butter (2 tablespoons)

Italian Fontina cheese (4 ounces)

Unsalted shelled pistachios (¼ cup)

From the Pantry

Kosher salt

Black pepper

Roasted Corn and Avocado Salad

6 SERVINGS TIME: 50 MINUTES

This is one of our favorite warm-weather salads and a real crowd-pleaser. We love summer corn at its peak, and roasting it with paprika gives it a delightful kick. The sweet corn, along with fresh, bright cherry tomatoes, creamy avocado, and fresh basil, is the essence of summer on a plate.

5 tablespoons extra-virgin olive oil

¼ teaspoon paprika

Kosher salt

Freshly ground black pepper

6 ears corn, husks and silk removed

1½ cups cherry tomatoes, halved

⅓ cup finely chopped red onion

¼ cup fresh basil leaves, very thinly sliced (see chiffonade, page 26)

2 tablespoons sherry vinegar

1 ripe avocado, cut into small cubes

1. Preheat the oven to 450°F.

2. In a small bowl, combine 3 tablespoons of the olive oil, the paprika, ¼ teaspoon salt, and ⅛ teaspoon pepper. Mix to incorporate. Using a pastry brush, spread the oil mixture on each of the ears of corn and wrap them individually in aluminum foil. Place the corn on a rimmed baking sheet and roast for 30 to 35 minutes, turning several times, until just tender.

3. Remove the corn from the foil and let cool. Once cooled, cut the kernels off the cob.

4. In a medium bowl, toss together the corn, 1 cup of the tomatoes, the onion, and basil until combined. Add the remaining 2 tablespoons olive oil and the vinegar and season with salt and pepper. Mix well.

5. Top with the remaining tomatoes and the avocado and serve.

From the Market

Corn (6 ears)

Cherry tomatoes (8 ounces)

Red onion (1 small)

Fresh basil (1 bunch)

Avocado (1 ripe)

From the Pantry

Extra-virgin olive oil (5 tablespoons)

Paprika (¼ teaspoon)

Kosher salt

Black pepper

Sherry vinegar (2 tablespoons)

Rice Noodle Nests

MAKES 16 NESTS   TIME: 1 HOUR

We originally came up with the idea for these Rice Noodle Nests because we were looking for an alternative to rice or noodles to serve with our Vegetarian Mapo Tofu with Spinach (page 118) and our Dry-Fried Beef with Vegetables (page 196). We ended up loving them so much, and realized they were quite versatile. We started serving them with many different stir-fries, as a base for a fried egg sandwich, and even in place of a bun for our burgers.

2 tablespoons coconut oil,
plus extra for greasing

One 8-ounce package pad thai noodles
(we like brown rice noodles)

2 large eggs

1 tablespoon all-purpose flour

Kosher salt

1. Grease a 12-cup muffin tin and 4 wells of a second muffin tin with coconut oil. (Alternatively, use moon pie or whoopie pie pans.)

2. Bring a large pot of water to a boil over high heat. Do not salt the water. Add the noodles and cook according to the directions on the package. Drain and rinse the noodles and set aside.

3. In a large bowl, whisk together the eggs, flour, and ¼ teaspoon salt until blended. Add the cooked noodles and mix thoroughly until well coated (your hands work best for this).

4. Fill the bottoms of the oiled tins with the noodles, using about ¼ cup per mold. Press the noodles firmly into the bottoms of the cups and cover with plastic wrap. Using a can or jar, firmly push down on each nest to press the noodles together. Freeze the pans for 15 minutes or refrigerate for at least 30 minutes or up to 8 hours.

5. Preheat the oven to 300°F.

6. In a large nonstick skillet over medium heat, melt 1 tablespoon of the coconut oil and heat until shimmering. Working in batches, use a plastic spatula or plastic knife to remove the nests from the muffin tins and gently place them in the skillet.

7. Cook undisturbed until golden brown, about 3 minutes. Flip the nests and cook until golden brown, about 3 minutes more. Season lightly with salt. Transfer to a rimmed baking sheet and place in the oven to keep warm until serving. Wipe the skillet clean, add the remaining 1 tablespoon of coconut oil, and repeat with the remaining nests.

From the Market

Pad thai noodles
(one 8-ounce package)

Large eggs (2)

From the Pantry

All-purpose flour
(1 tablespoon)

Kosher salt

Coconut oil
(2 tablespoons, plus extra
for greasing)

Gluten-free: use gluten-free flour in place of all-purpose flour.

CHAPTER 10

DIY

Tortilla Chips

MAKES 40   TIME: 15 MINUTES

4 cups vegetable oil, or as needed,
for frying

10 corn tortillas, each sliced into 4 wedges

Sea salt

1. Line a rimmed baking sheet with paper towel and set it nearby.

2. Pour the vegetable oil into a deep, high-sided skillet to a depth of at least 1 inch (use more or less as needed) and heat the oil over medium-high heat. (To determine if the oil is hot enough, insert the handle of a wooden spoon. If bubbles form around the wood and begin to float, the oil is ready.) Add a handful of the tortilla wedges to the oil, being careful not to overcrowd the pan, and fry until golden, about 1½ minutes. Using tongs, flip the tortillas and fry for an additional 1½ to 2 minutes, until the tortillas are crisp and golden brown. Using the tongs or a slotted spoon, remove the tortilla chips from the oil and place them on the paper towel–lined baking sheet to drain. Repeat with the remaining tortilla wedges.

3. Sprinkle with salt and serve, or let cool completely, then store in an airtight container at room temperature for up to 1 week.

From the Market
Corn tortillas (10)

From the Pantry
Vegetable oil (1 quart)
Sea salt

Pickled Red Onions

MAKES ABOUT 1½ CUPS   TIME: 35 MINUTES

1 large red onion, halved lengthwise, then sliced into thin half-moons

½ cup red wine vinegar

½ cup apple cider vinegar

¼ cup granulated sugar

Sea salt

1 large jalapeño pepper, sliced into thin rounds

½ teaspoon whole black peppercorns

1. Place the onion in a heat-resistant bowl.

2. In a small saucepan over high heat, combine the vinegars. Add the sugar, 1 teaspoon salt, and the jalapeño pepper. Heat, stirring occasionally, until the sugar has dissolved, 2 to 3 minutes. Pour the vinegar mixture over the onion, add the peppercorns, and cover. Set aside and let cool to room temperature, 20 to 30 minutes.

3. Transfer the onion and pickling liquid to a glass jar and store in the refrigerator for up to 2 weeks.

From the Market

Red onion (1 large)

Jalapeño pepper (1 large)

From the Pantry

Red wine vinegar (½ cup)

Apple cider vinegar (½ cup)

Granulated sugar (¼ cup)

Sea salt

Black peppercorns (½ teaspoon)

Vegan: use turbinado sugar in place of granulated.

Mango Chutney

MAKES FIVE 6-OUNCE JARS   TIME: 1 HOUR 15 MINUTES

1¼ cups granulated sugar

1 cup white vinegar

4 cups chopped peeled ripe mangoes (½-inch pieces)

1 cup finely chopped yellow onion

½ cup finely chopped red bell pepper

½ cup golden raisins

1 tablespoon grated fresh ginger

1 clove garlic, minced

½ teaspoon yellow mustard seeds

¼ teaspoon crushed red pepper flakes, or to taste

Kosher salt

In a large pot, combine the sugar and white vinegar and bring to a boil. Cook, stirring, until the sugar has dissolved, about 3 minutes. Add the mangoes, onion, bell pepper, raisins, ginger, garlic, mustard seeds, red pepper flakes, and ½ teaspoon salt and stir to combine. Reduce the heat to low and simmer, stirring occasionally, until thickened and syrupy, 45 to 55 minutes. Remove from the heat and let cool. Pour into 6-ounce glass jars and store in the refrigerator for up to 4 months.

From the Market

Ripe mangoes (3 or 4 large)

Red bell pepper (1 small)

Yellow onion (1 small)

Garlic (1 clove)

Fresh ginger (1 knob)

Golden raisins (½ cup)

Yellow mustard seeds (½ teaspoon)

From the Pantry

Granulated sugar (1¼ cups)

White vinegar (1 cup)

Crushed red pepper flakes (¼ teaspoon)

Kosher salt

Vegan: use coconut sugar in place of granulated.

Poblano Tahini Sauce

1½ cups roughly chopped poblano peppers

1 clove garlic, quartered

⅓ cup tahini (sesame paste)

3 tablespoons fresh lemon juice

1 tablespoon extra-virgin olive oil

½ teaspoon sea salt

⅛ teaspoon freshly ground black pepper

1. Combine all the ingredients in a blender or food processor, add ¼ cup water, and blend until smooth. If the mixture is too thick, add additional water as needed to reach the desired consistency.

2. Store in an airtight container in the refrigerator for up to 1 week.

From the Market
Poblano peppers (2 medium)
Garlic (1 clove)
Lemon (1)

From the Pantry
Tahini (⅓ cup)
Extra-virgin olive oil
(1 tablespoon)
Sea salt
Black pepper

Pico de Gallo

MAKES 2½ CUPS   TIME: 15 MINUTES

1¼ pounds ripe tomatoes, chopped

⅓ cup finely chopped red onion

2 teaspoons chopped fresh cilantro (optional)

1 teaspoon finely chopped jalapeño pepper, or to taste

1 tablespoon fresh lime juice

¾ teaspoon sea salt

⅛ teaspoon freshly ground black pepper

In a medium bowl, stir together all the ingredients. Store in an airtight container in the refrigerator for up to 1 week.

From the Market

Ripe tomatoes
(1¼ pounds)

Red onion (1 small)

Fresh cilantro
(1 small bunch; optional)

Jalapeño pepper (1)

Lime (1)

From the Pantry

Sea salt

Black pepper

Teriyaki Sauce

MAKES ¾ CUP TIME: 20 MINUTES

½ cup low-sodium soy sauce

2 tablespoons mirin

2 tablespoons dark brown sugar

1 clove garlic, minced

1 teaspoon grated fresh ginger

1 teaspoon cornstarch, dissolved in
2 teaspoons cold water

1 teaspoon toasted sesame oil

1. In a small saucepan, combine the soy sauce, mirin, brown sugar, garlic, ginger, and ⅓ cup water. Bring to a low boil over medium-high heat, stirring occasionally. Reduce the heat to medium and add the cornstarch mixture. Cook, stirring, until the sauce thickens slightly, 3 to 5 minutes. Remove from the heat and stir in the sesame oil.

2. Let cool completely, then transfer to an airtight container. Store in the refrigerator for up to 1 week or in the freezer for up to 3 months.

From the Market
Ginger (1 small knob)
Garlic (1 clove)

From the Pantry
Cornstarch (1 teaspoon)
Low-sodium soy sauce (½ cup)
Mirin (2 tablespoons)
Dark brown sugar (2 tablespoons)
Toasted sesame oil (1 teaspoon)

Vegan: use coconut sugar in place of brown sugar. Gluten-free: use tamari in place of soy sauce.

Roasted Tomatillo Salsa

MAKES 2¾ CUPS TIME: 20 MINUTES

1 pound tomatillos, husked, thoroughly rinsed, and dried

1 jalapeño pepper (2 for spicy salsa), stemmed

¼ cup fresh cilantro, thick stems removed

¼ cup finely chopped white onion

Sea salt

Freshly ground black pepper

1. Set a rack in the highest part of the oven (about 4 inches from the broiler) and preheat the oven to broil. Line a rimmed baking sheet with aluminum foil.

2. Place the tomatillos and jalapeño on the prepared baking sheet. Broil for 5 to 8 minutes, until the tops are charred. Flip the tomatillos and jalapeño and broil until their skins have black splotches and are blistered, 5 to 8 minutes more. Remove from the oven and let cool slightly.

3. In a food processor or blender, combine the tomatillos and jalapeño, any accumulated juices from the baking sheet, the cilantro, and ¼ cup water. Pulse until pureed.

4. Transfer to a bowl and add the onion, ½ teaspoon salt, and ⅛ teaspoon black pepper. Let cool to room temperature and transfer to an airtight container. Store in the refrigerator for up to 1 week or in the freezer for up to 1 month.

From the Market
Tomatillos (1 pound)
White onion (1 small)
Jalapeño pepper (1 or 2)
Fresh cilantro (1 small bunch)

From the Pantry
Sea salt
Black pepper

Classic Vegetable Broth

MAKES 2½ TO 3 QUARTS   TIME: 1 HOUR 50 MINUTES

1½ tablespoons extra-virgin olive oil

10 celery stalks, roughly chopped into 1-inch pieces

8 ounces white button mushrooms, quartered

5 large cloves garlic, unpeeled, halved

3 large carrots, roughly chopped into 1-inch pieces

2 large Spanish onions, unpeeled, roughly chopped into 1-inch pieces

2 leeks, thoroughly rinsed, white and pale green parts only, roughly chopped into 1-inch pieces

2 large shallots, roughly chopped into 1-inch pieces

1 small red bell pepper, roughly chopped into 1-inch pieces

½ cup dry white wine

2 tablespoons low-sodium soy sauce

8 sprigs fresh flat-leaf parsley

4 sprigs fresh thyme

2 bay leaves

1. In a large stockpot over medium heat, heat the olive oil until shimmering. Add the celery, mushrooms, garlic, carrots, onion, leeks, shallot, and bell pepper and cook, stirring occasionally, until the vegetables begin to soften, about 10 minutes. Add the wine, soy sauce, and 4 quarts water. Add the parsley, thyme, and bay leaves and bring the water to a boil. Reduce the heat to low and simmer, partially covered, stirring occasionally, for 1 hour.

2. Remove the pot from the heat. Set a fine mesh strainer over a large bowl. Strain the broth and let cool. Transfer the broth to airtight containers and store in the refrigerator for up to 1 week or in the freezer for up to 6 months.

From the Market

Celery (10 stalks)

Red bell pepper (1 small)

Carrots (3 large)

White button mushrooms (8 ounces)

Leeks (2)

Shallots (2 large)

Spanish onions (2 large)

Garlic (5 large cloves)

Fresh thyme (4 sprigs)

Fresh flat-leaf parsley (1 small bunch)

From the Pantry

Extra-virgin olive oil (1½ tablespoons)

Dry white wine (½ cup)

Low-sodium soy sauce (2 tablespoons)

Bay leaves (2)

Gluten-free: use tamari in place of soy sauce.

CHAPTER 11

Sweets

Apple Galette Rustique
with Apricot Glaze

8 SERVINGS   TIME: 1 HOUR 30 MINUTES

A galette is a flat, rustic fruit pie—the more freeform it looks, the greater its charm. This crust is flaky and sweet and almost melts in your mouth. Think of this dish as a lighter, easier, and yet more impressive version of a traditional apple pie.

FOR THE CRUST

1½ cups all-purpose flour, plus extra for dusting

2 tablespoons granulated sugar

¼ teaspoon kosher salt

¾ cup (1½ sticks) unsalted butter, very well chilled, cut into cubes

4 tablespoons ice-cold water, or more if needed

FOR THE GALETTE

4 medium Golden Delicious apples (about 1½ pounds)

½ teaspoon finely grated lemon zest

1 tablespoon fresh lemon juice

1 teaspoon ground cinnamon

3 tablespoons plus 2 teaspoons turbinado sugar

1 tablespoon all-purpose flour

1 teaspoon unsalted butter, chilled

1 tablespoon whole or low-fat milk

FOR THE GLAZE

2 tablespoons apricot preserves

1 tablespoon Cointreau, Grand Marnier, or Calvados liqueur

FOR THE CRUST:

1. Place a rolling pin in the freezer.

2. In a medium mixing bowl, combine the flour, granulated sugar, and salt and whisk together. Add the butter cubes and, using a pastry cutter or two forks, cut the butter into the flour mixture until the butter pieces are the size of peas.

3. Begin to add the ice water to the dough, 1 tablespoon at a time, gently mixing the dough with your hands after each addition until the dough forms small clumps and can be pinched together. Shape the dough into a rough ball, place on a piece of plastic wrap, and flatten into a disk. Cover the dough with the plastic wrap and refrigerate for at least 30 minutes.

FOR THE GALETTE:

4. Set a rack in the middle of the oven and preheat the oven to 400°F.

5. Peel, quarter, and core the apples. Cut the quarters into ⅛-inch-thick slices and place in a medium mixing bowl. Add the lemon zest, lemon juice, cinnamon, and 2 tablespoons of the turbinado sugar and gently stir to combine.

6. In a small bowl, combine the flour and 1 tablespoon of the turbinado sugar and mix.

Continued

7. Lightly flour a piece of parchment paper. Remove the dough from the refrigerator and place it on top. Cover the disk with another piece of parchment. Remove the rolling pin from the freezer and begin to roll out the dough from the center out, turning as you roll to create a uniform circle. Continue rolling until you have a 13-inch disk about ⅛ inch thick. Transfer the parchment paper with the dough disk to a rimmed baking sheet and then remove the top parchment sheet.

8. Sprinkle the flour-sugar mixture over the rolled dough and begin to arrange the apple slices on top. Working in either rows or concentric circles, overlap the slices by half, leaving a 1½-inch border around the edges. Fold the edges toward the center, overlapping when necessary, and pinch gently to seal any cracks to prevent the juices from leaking.

9. Cut the butter into slivers and dot them over the filling. Brush a thin coating of milk over the folded edges of the dough and sprinkle them with the remaining 2 teaspoons turbinado sugar.

10. Bake for 25 minutes. Reduce the oven temperature to 375°F, rotate the baking sheet, and bake until the crust is deep golden brown, an additional 10 to 15 minutes.

FOR THE GLAZE:

11. In a small saucepan over medium-low heat, heat the preserves and liqueur until warm, about 2 minutes. Strain through a sieve to remove any chunks and set aside.

12. Remove the galette from the oven and transfer it on the parchment paper to a wire rack. Using a large spatula or a knife, carefully lift the hot galette and slide the parchment out from underneath (to prevent the crust from becoming soggy).

13. Brush the apples with the glaze and serve warm.

From the Market

Golden Delicious apples, 4 medium (about 1½ pounds)

Lemon (1)

Unsalted butter (¾ cup or 1½ sticks, plus 1 teaspoon)

Milk, whole or low-fat (1 tablespoon)

Apricot preserves (2 tablespoons)

Cointreau, Grand Marnier, or Calvados liqueur (1 mini bottle or 1 tablespoon)

From the Pantry

All-purpose flour (1½ cups and 1 tablespoon, plus more for dusting)

Granulated sugar (2 tablespoons)

Kosher salt (¼ teaspoon)

Ground cinnamon (1 teaspoon)

Turbinado sugar (3 tablespoons plus 2 teaspoons)

*You will need parchment paper.

Banana-Loaded Cream Pie
with Chocolate Swirls

6 TO 8 SERVINGS   TIME: 45 MINUTES PLUS 3 HOURS CHILLING

Whatever happened to banana cream pie? Growing up, nine times out of ten that was the dessert we would order whenever it was on a menu. We decided we needed to create our own version—a delectably rich and creamy one, brimming with bananas on a crispy graham cracker crust. We couldn't resist topping it off with swirls of chocolate. Pure heaven.

FOR THE CRUST

1½ cups finely crushed graham crackers (10 to 12 full sheets)

2 tablespoons granulated sugar

¼ teaspoon kosher salt

5 tablespoons unsalted butter, melted

FOR THE FILLING

¾ cup granulated sugar

¼ cup cornstarch

2 cups half-and-half

4 large egg yolks

3 tablespoons unsalted butter, cut into cubes

1½ teaspoons pure vanilla extract

4 bananas

FOR THE WHIPPED CREAM TOPPING

1½ cups heavy cream, chilled

1½ teaspoons granulated sugar

½ teaspoon pure vanilla extract

FOR THE CHOCOLATE SAUCE (OPTIONAL)

½ cup half-and-half

1 tablespoon unsalted butter

8 ounces semisweet chocolate chips

½ teaspoon pure vanilla extract

FOR THE CRUST:

1. Set a rack in the middle of the oven and preheat the oven to 350°F.

2. In a medium mixing bowl, stir together the graham cracker crumbs, sugar, salt, and melted butter until well blended. Press evenly over the bottom and up the sides of a 9-inch pie pan. Bake, rotating the pan halfway through, until dry to the touch, 8 to 10 minutes. Remove from the oven and set aside to cool.

FOR THE FILLING:

3. In a medium saucepan, combine the sugar and cornstarch. Add the half-and-half and egg yolks and whisk until well combined. Bring to a boil over medium heat, stirring continuously, and boil for 1 minute, then remove from the heat. Stir in the butter and vanilla.

4. Pour half the filling into the cooled crust.

5. Slice 2 of the bananas and cover the filling in the crust with the banana slices. Pour the remaining filling over the bananas. Cover with plastic wrap, pressing it directly against the filling to keep a skin from forming. Chill for at least 3 hours or up to overnight.

6. Slice the 2 remaining bananas and arrange them over the filling, reserving a few slices for garnish. *Continued*

FOR THE WHIPPED CREAM:

7. Place the bowl and whisk attachment of a stand mixer (or a large metal bowl and a whisk, or beaters for a handheld mixer) in the freezer for at least 20 minutes.

8. Place the heavy cream, sugar, and vanilla in the chilled bowl and beat on low speed for 30 seconds, then increase the speed to medium and beat for an additional 30 seconds. Increase the speed to high and beat until the cream has doubled in volume and stiff peaks form, an additional 1 to 2 minutes. (The whipped cream can be prepared ahead, tightly covered with plastic wrap, and stored in the refrigerator for up to 1 day. If the cream separates, whip it again to reincorporate the liquid.)

9. Spread the whipped cream over the bananas and garnish the center of the pie with the reserved banana slices.

FOR THE CHOCOLATE SAUCE (OPTIONAL):

10. In a small heavy-bottomed saucepan over medium heat, heat the half-and-half and butter until small bubbles begin to form around the edge of the pan, 3 to 4 minutes (do not allow the cream to boil). Remove the pan from the heat.

11. Place the chocolate chips and vanilla in a medium heatproof bowl, add the hot half-and-half mixture, and let it rest for 2 minutes. Whisk until creamy.

12. Pour the chocolate sauce into a pastry bag (or a plastic bag with a small hole in one corner) and pipe swirls of chocolate over the top of the pie.

From the Market

Bananas (4 large)

Graham crackers
(10 to 12 full cracker sheets)

Unsalted butter
(½ cup or 1 stick, plus 1 tablespoon)

Half-and-half (2½ cups)

Heavy cream (1½ cups)

Large eggs (4)

From the Pantry

Granulated sugar (1 cup)

Kosher salt (¼ teaspoon)

Cornstarch (¼ cup)

Semisweet chocolate chips
(1¼ cups)

Vanilla extract, pure (2½ teaspoons)

Basil-Infused Strawberry Shortcake

8 SERVINGS TIME: 45 MINUTES

This is our updated take on the classic summer dessert. In our rendition, buttery, flaky shortcake biscuits are paired with juicy strawberries infused with slightly sweet, aromatic basil. We top it off with a generous dollop of homemade whipped cream. This will become your go-to treat for summer.

FOR THE STRAWBERRIES

4 cups sliced fresh strawberries

2 tablespoons sugar

6 fresh basil leaves, very thinly sliced (see chiffonade, page 26), plus 8 small whole leaves for garnish

FOR THE SHORTCAKES

2 cups all-purpose flour

2 tablespoons plus 1½ teaspoons granulated sugar

1 tablespoon baking powder

½ teaspoon kosher salt

½ cup (1 stick) unsalted butter, cut into small cubes and chilled

2 large eggs, at room temperature, lightly beaten

½ cup heavy cream, chilled

1 large egg white, lightly beaten, for the egg wash

FOR THE WHIPPED CREAM

1 cup heavy cream

2 tablespoons granulated sugar

1 teaspoon pure vanilla extract

1. Place a medium metal mixing bowl and the beaters for a handheld mixer (or a metal whisk) in the freezer for at least 20 minutes.

2. Set a rack in the middle of the oven and preheat the oven to 425°F. Line a rimmed baking sheet with parchment paper.

FOR THE STRAWBERRIES:

3. Place 1 cup of the strawberries in a medium mixing bowl and gently crush with a fork to release their juices. Add the remaining 3 cups strawberries, the sugar, and the basil chiffonade and mix with a wooden spoon. Set aside for about 30 minutes to develop the flavor.

FOR THE SHORTCAKES:

4. Sift the flour, the 2 tablespoons of sugar, the baking powder, and salt into a medium mixing bowl.

5. Add the butter cubes to the flour mixture. Working with your fingers or a pastry blender, gently cut the butter into the flour until it resembles coarse meal. Add the whole eggs and heavy cream and incorporate (your hands work well for this). The dough will be sticky.

6. Flour a work surface and turn the dough out onto it. Flour your hands and pat the dough into a ¾-inch-thick rectangle. Using a 3-inch biscuit cutter, cut out 6 rounds. Place 1 inch apart on the prepared baking sheet. Gently gather the dough

Continued

scraps together and pat them into a ¾-inch-thick rectangle. Cut out 2 rounds and set them on the baking sheet with the others. Brush the tops of each biscuit with the egg wash and sprinkle with the remaining 1½ teaspoons sugar.

7. Bake until the biscuits are lightly golden brown, 12 to 14 minutes, rotating the baking sheet halfway through. Place the baking sheet on a wire rack and let cool.

FOR THE WHIPPED CREAM:

8. Meanwhile, in the chilled bowl using the chilled beaters or whisk, beat the cream, sugar, and vanilla on low speed until well blended.

Increase the speed to high and beat until firm peaks form, about 2 minutes. Refrigerate until ready to use.

9. To assemble the strawberry shortcakes, cut each biscuit in half crosswise. Spoon a generous portion of the strawberries onto the bottom halves and a dollop of whipped cream onto each. Place the biscuit tops over the whipped cream. Garnish each shortcake with a spoonful of the whipped cream and a basil leaf, and serve.

From the Market
Strawberries
(1 quart or 1½ pounds)
Fresh basil (1 small bunch)
Unsalted butter
(½ cup or 1 stick)

Large eggs (3)
Heavy cream (1½ cups)

From the Pantry
Granulated sugar
(6 tablespoons plus 1½ teaspoons)
All-purpose flour (2 cups)

Baking powder (1 tablespoon)
Kosher salt (½ teaspoon)
Vanilla extract, pure (1 teaspoon)
*You will need parchment paper.

Chocolate Nocciola Cookie Crisps

MAKES 2½ TO 3 DOZEN COOKIES TIME: 1 HOUR PLUS 2 HOURS CHILLING

We first thought of the idea for these cookies while eating two scoops of gelato—one hazelnut, one chocolate—at a gelateria in Florence. There is just something magical about the combination of chocolate and hazelnut, and we think we've captured that magic here. Warning: These crisp little treats are habit-forming!

1½ cups all-purpose flour

½ cup granulated sugar

½ cup confectioners' sugar

½ cup unsweetened cocoa powder

¼ cup cornmeal

½ teaspoon kosher salt

¼ teaspoon baking soda

1 cup (2 sticks) unsalted butter, cut into cubes and chilled

1½ teaspoons pure vanilla extract

½ cup chocolate-hazelnut spread (see Note)

1 ounce unsweetened chocolate, melted and cooled

1. In a food processor, combine the flour, sugars, cocoa powder, cornmeal, salt, and baking soda and pulse until combined. Add the butter and vanilla and pulse until the mixture has a sand-like consistency. Add the hazelnut spread and melted chocolate and pulse until the dough forms. Divide the dough into 2 pieces. Flatten them into disks and wrap in plastic. Refrigerate for 2 hours.

2. Set racks in the upper- and lower-third of the oven and preheat to 325°F. Line two baking sheets with parchment paper.

3. Remove the dough from the refrigerator and transfer it to a work surface. You may need to let the dough rest for 5 to 10 minutes if it is too firm to work with.

4. Between two sheets of parchment paper, roll out each disk of dough ¼ inch thick. Using a 2½-inch cookie cutter or the rim of a glass, cut cookies out of the rolled dough and place on the prepared baking sheets 1 inch apart. Gather the dough scraps, reroll between the parchment sheets, and cut out more cookies, repeating this step as necessary and transferring the cookies to the prepared baking sheets.

5. Bake the cookies for 12 to 15 minutes, until the tops are firm. Let cool for 5 minutes on the baking sheet, then transfer to a wire cooling rack to finish cooling. Store in an airtight container.

Note: Preferably use a chocolate-hazelnut spread that doesn't contain palm oil.

From the Market

Unsweetened cocoa powder (½ cup)

Unsalted butter (1 cup or 2 sticks)

Chocolate-hazelnut spread (½ cup)

Unsweetened chocolate (1 ounce)

From the Pantry

All-purpose flour (1½ cups)

Granulated sugar (½ cup)

Confectioners' sugar (½ cup)

Cornmeal (¼ cup)

Kosher salt (½ teaspoon)

Baking soda (¼ teaspoon)

Vanilla extract, pure (1½ teaspoons)

*You will need parchment paper.

Piña Colada Crumble

6 TO 8 SERVINGS   TIME: 1 HOUR 20 MINUTES

Crumbles are a breeze to assemble and can be made with just about any fruit or combination of fruits. Berry, peach, and apple are traditional crumble flavors, but we think we've taken this classic dessert to a new level with our piña colada version. The mix of bananas, pineapple, and coconut evokes everyone's favorite tropical drink.

FOR THE FILLING

1 medium pineapple, peeled, cored, and cut into ½-inch cubes (about 5½ cups)

3 ripe but firm bananas, cut into ½-inch slices

¼ cup granulated sugar

¼ cup unsweetened coconut flakes

2 tablespoons quick-cooking tapioca (or all-purpose flour)

1 tablespoon fresh lime juice

1 teaspoon finely grated fresh ginger

1 teaspoon ground cinnamon

¼ teaspoon ground nutmeg

⅛ teaspoon kosher salt

FOR THE CRUMBLE TOPPING

1 cup all-purpose flour

1 cup old-fashioned rolled oats (not instant)

1 cup firmly packed dark brown sugar

½ teaspoon ground cinnamon

⅛ teaspoon kosher salt

½ cup (1 stick) unsalted butter, cut into small cubes and chilled

1. Set a rack in the middle of the oven and preheat the oven to 375°F.

FOR THE FILLING:

2. Place the pineapple and bananas in a large mixing bowl. Add the granulated sugar, coconut flakes, tapioca, lime juice, ginger, cinnamon, nutmeg, and salt and gently toss to combine.

Spoon the filling into an ungreased 9-inch round or 11-inch oval 2-inch-deep pie dish.

FOR THE CRUMBLE TOPPING:

3. In a medium mixing bowl, whisk together the flour, rolled oats, brown sugar, cinnamon, and salt. Add the butter and, working with your fingers, a fork, or pastry blender, work the butter into the flour mixture until the crumbs are pea-size.

4. Spoon the topping evenly but thickly over the fruit filling.

5. Place the pie pan on a baking sheet or a sheet of aluminum foil (this will catch any spills). Bake until the fruit is bubbling and the top is nicely browned, 45 to 50 minutes. To ensure even baking, rotate the pie halfway through. If the top begins to get too brown, cover with a sheet of aluminum foil. Serve warm.

Food for Thought

Pineapple is not only a delicious tropical fruit, but it also has enormous health benefits. Pineapples contain an enzyme called bromelain, which is primarily associated with breaking down complex protein and has natural anti-inflammatory effects. One cup of pineapple also provides 100 percent of the daily requirement of vitamin C.

From the Market

Pineapple (1 medium)

Bananas (3 ripe but firm)

Lime (1)

Fresh ginger (1 knob)

Unsalted butter (½ cup or 1 stick)

Quick-cooking tapioca
(2 tablespoons)

Unsweetened coconut flakes
(¼ cup)

From the Pantry

Granulated sugar (¼ cup)

Ground cinnamon (1½ teaspoons)

Ground nutmeg (¼ teaspoon)

Kosher salt (¼ teaspoon)

All-purpose flour (1 cup, plus
an additional 2 tablespoons if not
using tapioca)

Old-fashioned rolled oats (1 cup)

Dark brown sugar (1 cup)

Blueberry Nectarine Buckle

8 TO 10 SERVINGS   TIME: 1 HOUR

This buckle is, in essence, a fruit-filled coffee cake. The slightly tart blueberries and juicy, sweet nectarines are a winning combination. Buttery and moist, we love this cake right out of the oven, but we've also been known to indulge in a slice with our morning coffee the next day.

½ cup (1 stick) unsalted butter,
at room temperature, plus extra for greasing

2 cups sliced peeled nectarines (or substitute
1 pound frozen sliced nectarines or peaches,
thawed and patted dry with a tea towel or
paper towel)

½ cup granulated sugar

1 teaspoon fresh lemon juice

¼ cup light brown sugar

3 large eggs, at room temperature

1 teaspoon pure vanilla extract

Zest of 1 lemon

1¼ cups all-purpose flour

½ teaspoon kosher salt

½ teaspoon ground nutmeg

¼ teaspoon baking powder

2 cups blueberries

1 tablespoon turbinado sugar

1. Preheat the oven to 375°F. Butter a 9-inch baking dish or cake pan.

2. Place the nectarine slices in a medium saucepan over medium heat. Add ¼ cup of the granulated sugar and the lemon juice. Bring to a simmer and cook, stirring continuously, for 4 to 5 minutes. Remove from the heat and set aside. (If using frozen nectarines or peaches, use a slotted spoon to transfer the fruit to a bowl and continue to cook the juices until slightly thickened, 2 to 3 minutes more. Add the juices to the bowl with the cooked fruit and set aside to cool.)

3. In a large mixing bowl, or in the bowl of a stand mixer fitted with a paddle attachment, beat the butter, the remaining ¼ cup granulated sugar, and the brown sugar on medium speed until light and fluffy, about 1 minute. Beat in the eggs one at a time. Add the vanilla and lemon zest and beat until well incorporated.

4. In a medium mixing bowl, combine the flour, salt, nutmeg, and baking powder and stir to combine. Add the dry ingredients to the wet and mix until just incorporated.

5. Fold the nectarines and their juices into the batter. Fold in the blueberries and gently mix. Pour the batter into the prepared baking dish and sprinkle with the turbinado sugar. Bake until golden brown and a cake tester inserted into the center comes out clean, 35 to 45 minutes. Serve warm.

From the Market

Fresh nectarines (2 medium) or
frozen sliced nectarines or peaches
(1 pound, thawed)

Blueberries (1 pint or 2 cups)

Lemon (1)

Unsalted butter (½ cup or 1 stick,
plus extra for greasing)

Large eggs
(3)

From the Pantry

Granulated sugar (½ cup)

Light brown sugar (¼ cup)

Vanilla extract, pure (1 teaspoon)

All-purpose flour (1¼ cups)

Kosher salt (½ teaspoon)

Ground nutmeg (½ teaspoon)

Baking powder (¼ teaspoon)

Turbinado sugar (1 tablespoon)

*You will need parchment paper.

West Tisbury Carrot Cake

MAKES ONE 9-INCH LAYER CAKE (8 TO 10 SERVINGS)   TIME: 2 HOURS

We are obsessed with this carrot cake. The recipe was originally given to us by a friend living in West Tisbury on Martha's Vineyard, and we made our own modifications over the years. The result is an incredibly moist, lightly spiced, carroty-nutty confection. The cake is finished with an ultra-rich cream cheese frosting. Perhaps we're a little biased, but we declare this the best carrot cake ever.

⅓ cup sweetened shredded coconut

2 cups raw walnuts

FOR THE CAKE

Unsalted butter, for greasing

2 cups all-purpose flour, plus extra for dusting

2 teaspoons baking soda

2 teaspoons baking powder

1 teaspoon kosher salt

1 teaspoon ground cinnamon

½ teaspoon ground cloves

1½ cups vegetable oil

1½ cups honey

4 large eggs, at room temperature

2 tablespoons plain whole-milk yogurt

1 teaspoon pure vanilla extract

2½ cups grated carrots

1 cup raisins

FOR THE FROSTING

One 8-ounce package cream cheese, at room temperature

½ cup (1 stick) butter, at room temperature

1 teaspoon pure vanilla extract

1 pound (about 3½ cups) confectioners' sugar

1. Set a rack in the middle of the oven and preheat the oven to 350°F. Line a rimmed baking sheet with a silicone baking mat or parchment paper.

2. Spread the shredded coconut on the prepared baking sheet. Spread the walnuts on a separate, unlined rimmed baking sheet. Put the baking sheet with the coconut in the oven and toast for 5 to 7 minutes, until lightly browned, flipping once halfway through. Remove from the oven, transfer to a plate, and let cool.

3. Place the baking sheet with the walnuts in the oven and toast for 8 to 10 minutes, until they give off a nutty aroma, flipping once halfway through. Remove from the oven, transfer to a separate plate, and let cool. Roughly chop 1½ cups for the cake. Finely chop the remaining ½ cup and set aside to decorate the frosting.

FOR THE CAKE:

4. Butter two 9-inch round cake pans. Line the bottom of the pans with parchment paper cut to fit. Butter the paper, then dust the pans with flour, tapping out any excess.

5. In a medium mixing bowl, sift together the flour, baking soda, baking powder, salt, cinnamon, and cloves. Set aside.

6. In a large mixing bowl using a handheld mixer, beat together the vegetable oil and honey until well combined. Beat in the eggs one at a time and

Continued

add the yogurt and vanilla. With the mixer on low speed, slowly add the dry ingredients to the wet until fully incorporated. Stir in the carrots, the 1½ cups roughly chopped walnuts, and the raisins.

7. Pour the batter into the prepared pans, dividing it equally. Bake for 40 to 45 minutes, rotating the pans front to back halfway through, until the cake is springy and a cake tester inserted in the center of each cake comes out clean. Transfer the pans to a wire cooling rack and let cool for 20 minutes. Run a knife around the sides of the cakes and invert them onto the wire rack. Remove the parchment and let cool completely, about 20 minutes more.

FOR THE FROSTING:

8. In a medium mixing bowl using a handheld mixer, beat the cream cheese and butter on medium speed until smooth, about 1 minute. Beat in the vanilla. Reduce the speed to low, gradually add the confectioners' sugar, mixing until smooth. Increase the speed to high and beat the frosting until light and fluffy, about 2 minutes.

9. Place one cake layer, flat-side up, on a serving plate. With a knife or icing spatula, very generously spread frosting over the top and sides. Place the second layer on top, rounded-side up, and spread frosting evenly over the top and sides. Sprinkle the top with the toasted coconut and the ½ cup finely chopped walnuts.

From the market

Carrots (2 large)

Unsalted butter
(½ cup or 1 stick, plus extra for greasing)

Large eggs (4)

Yogurt, plain whole-milk
(2 tablespoons)

Cream cheese
(one 8-ounce package)

Raisins (1 cup)

Sweetened shredded coconut
(⅓ cup)

From the Pantry

Raw walnuts (2 cups)

All-purpose flour
(2 cups, plus extra for dusting)

Baking soda (2 teaspoons)

Baking powder (2 teaspoons)

Kosher salt (1 teaspoon)

Ground cinnamon (1 teaspoon)

Ground cloves (½ teaspoon)

Vegetable oil (1½ cups)

Honey (1½ cups)

Vanilla extract, pure (2 teaspoons)

Confectioners' sugar (1 pound)

*You will need parchment paper.

Grandma Mary's Glazed Zucchini Cake

MAKES ONE 10-INCH BUNDT CAKE (10 TO 12 SERVINGS) TIME: 1 HOUR 35 MINUTES

We still remember the first time we had our grandmother Mary's zucchini cake. We couldn't believe that an ordinary vegetable could yield such a delicious dessert—wonderfully moist, delicately spiced, with a delightfully nutty texture. Mary didn't use written recipes, so we followed her around the kitchen and took notes. This is her recipe, with our own addition of a glaze. We tested both a vanilla and a lemon glaze—we couldn't decide which we loved more, so we decided to include both options here.

FOR THE CAKE

Unsalted butter, for greasing

3 large eggs, at room temperature

2 cups granulated sugar

1 cup vegetable oil

1 tablespoon pure vanilla extract

2 cups grated unpeeled zucchini, patted dry in a tea towel or paper towel

3 cups all-purpose flour

1 tablespoon ground cinnamon

1 teaspoon kosher salt

1 teaspoon baking soda

¼ teaspoon baking powder

1 cup chopped raw walnuts

FOR THE LEMON GLAZE

1 cup confectioners' sugar

2 tablespoons plus 1 teaspoon fresh lemon juice

1 teaspoon lemon zest

FOR THE VANILLA GLAZE

1 cup confectioners' sugar

2 tablespoons milk

½ teaspoon pure vanilla extract

FOR THE CAKE:

1. Set a rack in the middle of the oven and preheat the oven to 350°F. Generously grease a 10-inch Bundt pan with butter.

2. In a large mixing bowl using a handheld mixer or whisk, beat the eggs until light and foamy, about 1 minute. Add the granulated sugar, vegetable oil, and vanilla and beat for an additional minute to incorporate. Add the zucchini and mix well with a wooden spoon.

3. In a medium mixing bowl, combine the flour, cinnamon, salt, baking soda, and baking powder and stir until blended. Add the flour mixture to the batter a third at a time and mix until incorporated. Stir in the walnuts.

4. Pour the batter into the prepared pan. Bake, rotating the pan halfway through, until the cake is golden brown and a cake tester inserted into the center of the cake comes out clean, 55 to 60 minutes. Set the pan on a wire cooling rack to cool for 20 minutes.

FOR THE GLAZE:

5. Sift the confectioners' sugar into a medium mixing bowl. Add the lemon juice (for the lemon

Continued

glaze) or the milk and vanilla (for the vanilla glaze) and mix with a wire whisk until completely smooth.

6. Line a rimmed baking sheet with waxed paper or parchment paper and place a wire rack on top.

7. Invert the cake onto the wire rack and spoon the glaze on top of the cake, allowing the glaze to run down the sides. Sprinkle the top with the lemon zest if using the lemon glaze. Transfer to a cake plate and serve.

From the Market

Zucchini (2 small or 1 large)

Lemon (1; if making the lemon glaze)

Large eggs (3)

Milk (2 tablespoons; if making the vanilla glaze)

Unsalted butter (for greasing)

From the Pantry

Granulated sugar (2 cups)

Vegetable oil (1 cup)

Vanilla extract, pure
(1 tablespoon, plus ½ teaspoon if making vanilla glaze)

All-purpose flour (3 cups)

Ground cinnamon (1 tablespoon)

Kosher salt (1 teaspoon)

Baking soda (1 teaspoon)

Baking powder (¼ teaspoon)

Raw walnuts (1¼ cups)

Confectioners' sugar
(1 cup)
*You will need parchment paper.

Dairy-free: choose the lemon glaze and use vegetable oil in place of butter for greasing.

Caramelized Roasted Pears with Fresh Ricotta

4 SERVINGS TIME: 35 MINUTES

Nothing is simpler to make than these roasted pears with ricotta cheese, yet the result is pretty sensational. The pears, when cooked, turn soft and creamy, the balsamic vinegar adds sweet-tartness, and the drizzle of honey adds a floral note. The dollop of ricotta cheese is the perfect foil to all the lushness.

2 tablespoons unsalted butter

2 ripe but firm Bosc pears, halved lengthwise and cored

5 tablespoons balsamic vinegar

4 ounces fresh ricotta cheese

3 tablespoons honey

Freshly ground black pepper

1. Set a rack in the middle of the oven and preheat the oven to 400°F.

2. Place the butter in a 9 by 13-inch baking dish. Place the dish in the oven until the butter has melted, 2 to 3 minutes. Carefully remove from the oven and arrange the pears cut-side down in the melted butter. Roast the pears until tender, about 25 minutes.

3. Turn the pears cut-side up. Pour the vinegar over and roast for an additional 5 minutes.

4. Transfer the pears, cut-side up, to four serving plates. Spoon the juices from the baking dish over the pears and arrange 2 tablespoons of the cheese around each pear half. Drizzle the cheese and pears with honey, add freshly ground black pepper, and serve.

From the Market
Bosc pears (2 ripe but firm)
Unsalted butter (2 tablespoons)
Fresh ricotta cheese (4 ounces)

From the Pantry
Balsamic vinegar (5 tablespoons)
Honey (3 tablespoons)
Black pepper

Vegan Peanut Butter Salted Fudge Pops

6 TO 8 SERVINGS   TIME: 10 MINUTES PLUS 4 TO 5 HOURS FREEZING

One particularly hot August day, we were craving the Good Humor treats of our childhood and wanted to come up with our own modern, dairy-free version. These frosty chocolate–peanut butter delights are just the thing to help get you through those dog days of summer.

One 13.5-ounce can full-fat coconut milk

1 cup semisweet chocolate chips (vegan)

3 tablespoons natural creamy peanut butter

2 tablespoons agave nectar

1 teaspoon pure vanilla extract

Sea salt

Ice pop molds

6 to 8 ice pop sticks

1. Pour the coconut milk into a saucepan over medium heat. Add the chocolate chips, peanut butter, agave nectar, vanilla, and a pinch of salt. Stir until the ingredients are melted and well incorporated, 2 to 3 minutes. Pour into a large liquid measuring cup or pitcher.

2. Pour the fudge mixture into the molds and freeze for 30 minutes, then remove from the freezer and insert a stick into the center of each mold. Freeze until solid, at least 4 hours, before serving.

3. To remove a pop from the mold, fill a coffee mug with warm water and briefly submerge the mold. Pull the stick gently upward to release the pop.

From the Market

Coconut milk, full-fat
(one 13.5-ounce can)

Semisweet chocolate chips, vegan
(1 cup)

Peanut butter, natural creamy
(3 tablespoons)

Ice pop molds and sticks

From the Pantry

Agave nectar
(2 tablespoons)

Vanilla extract, pure
(1 teaspoon)

Sea salt

Elderflower Frosé After-Dinner Pops

MAKES 6 TO 8 POPS   TIME: 15 MINUTES PLUS 6 HOURS FREEZING

These ice pops are a refreshing grown-up treat. Crisp rosé wine and bright, fragrant elderberry liqueur are combined with fresh watermelon juice to create a sophisticated and pretty frozen cocktail dessert.

10 ounces seedless watermelon, cubed

1 cup rosé wine

¼ cup elderflower liqueur (such as St-Germain)

2 tablespoons agave nectar

2 tablespoons fresh lemon juice

Ice pop molds

6 to 8 ice pop sticks

1. Place the watermelon cubes in a blender and blend until smooth; strain, if desired. Add the rosé, elderflower liqueur, agave nectar, and lemon juice and blend. Pour the liquid into the molds and freeze for about 1 hour, until partially frozen, then insert a stick into the center of each pop. Freeze until solid, about 6 hours, before serving.

2. To remove a pop from the mold, fill a coffee mug with warm water and briefly submerge the mold. Pull the stick gently upward to release the pop.

From the Market

Rosé wine (1 cup)

Elderflower liqueur, such as St-Germain (¼ cup)

Watermelon, seedless (10 ounces)

Lemon (1)

Ice pop molds and sticks

From the Pantry

Agave nectar (2 tablespoons)

Wickedly Decadent
Chocolate Cake

MAKES ONE 9-INCH LAYER CAKE (8 TO 10 SERVINGS)   TIME: 1 HOUR 35 MINUTES

Intensely chocolaty and velvety smooth, our wicked layer cake is a chocolate lover's dream. Subtly flavored with coffee, this moist cake has a wonderfully complex flavor combination. This is the ultimate dessert to satisfy all your chocolate cravings.

FOR THE CAKE

Unsalted butter, for greasing

1¾ cups all-purpose flour, plus more for dusting

2 cups plus 2 tablespoons granulated sugar

¾ cup plus 2 tablespoons unsweetened cocoa powder

1½ teaspoons baking soda

1½ teaspoons baking powder

1 teaspoon kosher salt

2 large eggs, at room temperature

1 cup buttermilk

½ cup vegetable oil

1 teaspoon pure vanilla extract

¾ cup plus 2 tablespoons hot coffee

FOR THE CHOCOLATE CURLS

One 2-ounce chunk good-quality dark chocolate

FOR THE FROSTING

6 ounces semisweet chocolate, roughly chopped

1 cup (2 sticks) unsalted butter, at room temperature

1 teaspoon pure vanilla extract

1¼ cups sifted confectioners' sugar

FOR THE CAKE:

1. Set a rack in the middle of the oven and preheat the oven to 350°F. Butter two 9-inch round cake pans. Line the bottoms with parchment paper cut to fit and butter the paper, then dust the pans with flour, tapping out any excess.

2. In a large mixing bowl, whisk together the flour, granulated sugar, cocoa powder, baking soda, baking powder, and salt. Set aside.

3. In a separate bowl, whisk together the eggs, buttermilk, vegetable oil, and vanilla. Add the wet ingredients to the dry and stir with a wooden spoon until incorporated. Whisk in the hot coffee until just combined.

4. Divide the batter between the prepared pans and place them side by side in the oven. Bake until a cake tester inserted into the center of the cakes comes out clean, 30 to 35 minutes. Let cool in the pans on a wire cooling rack for 30 minutes, then invert the cakes onto the rack and let cool completely.

FOR THE CHOCOLATE CURLS:

5. Using a vegetable peeler, scrape the blade lengthwise across the dark chocolate chunk to create small curls and refrigerate until ready to use.

Continued

FOR THE FROSTING:

6. Place the semisweet chocolate in a heatproof bowl set over a saucepan of simmering water (be sure the bottom of the bowl does not touch the water). Stir until the chocolate has melted. Set aside to cool.

7. In the bowl of a stand mixer fitted with the paddle attachment or in a large mixing bowl using a handheld mixer, beat the butter on medium-high until fluffy, 2 to 3 minutes. Add the vanilla and beat for an additional minute. With the mixer on low, gradually add the confectioners' sugar, then beat on medium speed until smooth, scraping down the sides of the bowl as needed. With the mixer on low, add the melted chocolate and mix until just blended.

8. Remove the parchment paper from the cake. Place one cake layer, flat-side up, on a serving plate. With a knife or an icing spatula, spread the frosting over the top. Place the second layer, rounded-side up, on top. Frost the top and sides of the cake with the remaining frosting.

9. Remove the chocolate curls from the refrigerator and sprinkle them over the top of the cake.

From the Market

Unsalted butter (1 cup or 2 sticks, plus more for greasing)

Large eggs (2)

Buttermilk (1 cup)

Cocoa powder, unsweetened (¾ cup plus 2 tablespoons)

Coffee, brewed (¾ cup plus 2 tablespoons)

Dark chocolate, good-quality (one 2-ounce chunk)

Semisweet chocolate (6 ounces)

From the Pantry

Granulated sugar (2 cups plus 2 tablespoons)

All-purpose flour (1¾ cups)

Baking soda (1½ teaspoons)

Baking powder (1½ teaspoons)

Kosher salt (1 teaspoon)

Vegetable oil (½ cup)

Vanilla extract, pure (2 teaspoons)

Confectioners' sugar (1¼ cups)

*You will need parchment paper.

Acknowledgments

With love and gratitude, the four of us would like to express our heartfelt thanks to all the remarkable and talented people who helped shape our vision into a gorgeous and accessible cookbook.

Most important, thank you to our husbands and children. You encouraged us to write a second cookbook, perhaps forgetting how long and time-consuming the process is. You were our most enthusiastic and intrepid tasters and steadfast cheerleaders.

To Michael Pollan, our heartfelt thanks—you are our inspiration and best sounding board. Thank you for once again generously offering to write our foreword.

To our dear friend, the talented Lucy Kaylin—thank you for your insightful guidance and wonderful suggestions.

To Mitchell Stern, thank you for your invaluable legal and business counsel and dedication—we know you always have our collective back.

To Kari Stuart, our amazing agent—thank you for the passion you bring to our projects and your unwavering support. Thank you to Amanda Urban who is responsible for starting us on our literary path. Thank you also to Catherine Shook.

To Julie Will, our terrific editor, thank you for your enthusiasm and superb editing—your incredible talents brought this book to life. And thank you to our publisher, Karen Rinaldi, and the entire Harper Wave dream team: Milan Bozic, Leah Carlson-Stanisic, Yelena Nesbit, Penny Makras, Haley Swanson, and Brian Perrin.

To our brilliant photographer, Nicole Franzen, your artistic vision left us in awe—your photographs are more stunning than we could have ever imagined. Thank you for putting together a phenomenal creative team: food stylist, Carrie Purcell, prop stylist Kalen Kaminski, digital tech Will Wang, and assistants Judy Mancini, Lauren LaPenna, Lily Saporta Taguiri, and Nick Barranco.

To Judy Haubert, our indefatigable food tester—thank you for your excellent suggestions and attention to detail.

To Leslie Sloane and Jami Kandel, thank you for being extraordinary publicists.

To Mary Grieco, we can't thank you enough for your legal expertise and the generosity of your time. Thank you also to the infinitely resourceful Nina Tringali and the tireless and enthusiastic Amuna Ali, Nellie Vasquez, and Mabel James.

To Michael J. Fox, Judith Belzer, and Bob Friedman, thank you. Your support, insightful comments, and feedback were invaluable.

And finally our deepest thanks to each one of you who bought a copy of *Mostly Plants*; to all of our friends on social media; and to each person who has cooked our recipes. We love reading your comments and seeing the photos of the meals you have prepared, and we love your enthusiasm for good food. We are inspired by all of you.

Tracy

I owe tremendous gratitude for the love and encouragement of my husband, Michael, and my wonderful children Esmé, Schuyler, Aquinnah, and Sam. Creating and cooking new recipes is one of my most treasured activities and you are my favorite people to cook for. Your enthusiasm, constructive suggestions, and enormous support kept me going through this process. I am extraordinarily lucky to have a group of friends whose love, humor, and kindness mean the world to me. A special thank you to my siblings-in-law, Judith, Mitchell, and Bob, for joining and enriching the family table. Mom, Dana, Lori, and Mike, thank you doesn't begin to cover it. To have the opportunity to work together and cook together again has been a true blessing. Finally, thank you, Dad, for believing in me and teaching me to believe in myself. I love you and miss you every day.

Dana

To my husband and best friend, Mitchell Stern, thank you for your unfailing wisdom, support, and love. I'm so lucky to ride life's journey with you. Thank you to my children, Macklin, Savannah, and Cameron, for your love and inspiration. Your enthusiasm for the meals we share together, and seeing the wonderful cooks you have all become, brings me boundless joy. To Tracy, Lori, and Michael, I am eternally grateful for your friendship and love. Judith, Mike, and Bob, I feel truly blessed to have you as my family. Thank you to all my friends. I treasure each and every one of you and feel so fortunate to have you in my life. And thank you, Mom, for teaching me the valuable life skill of how to cook. I could not have written this book if it weren't for your encouragement and dedication. And Dad, I love you, and I know you are out there somewhere looking down at us, smiling.

Lori

Special thanks to all my wonderful, caring, and very fun friends. Your enthusiasm and excitement for both cookbooks touched me deeply. To Sam Standing, Ann Treesa, Zack, Lia, and Matthew—how lucky and blessed am I to have you awesome "extra children" in my life. I am eternally grateful for my incredible siblings and siblings-in-law, Michael, Tracy, Dana, Judith, Michael, and Mitchell—I am so fortunate to have not only your love but also your abiding friendship. I owe so much to my remarkable parents, Corky and Stephen, not just for their love and generosity but also their boundless and unwavering faith in me. My love and gratitude go to my husband and best friend, Bob—your kindness, encouragement, and stalwart support have meant more than words can say. Finally, to my three favorite people in the world, my children Hallie, Jack, and Mica—you are my joy and inspiration: All my love.

Corky

In loving thanks to my husband, Stephen, whose boundless enthusiasm for my embarking on a second book proved contagious. To my daughters, Lori, Tracy, and Dana, whose skills and talents continually amaze me—cooking and writing with them has been a sheer delight. To Judith Belzer, my other daughter, for her wise suggestions and loving support. To Mitchell Stern, who has always been there to lend a hand in countless ways. To Michael Fox, our resident wordsmith, who comes up with the absolute best words when we're momentarily stumped. To Bob Friedman, the newest member of the family, who has nimbly survived his introduction to the cookbook world. To my son, Michael, for his unwavering encouragement and generosity of time and spirit. To my grandchildren, many of whom have graduated from tasters to accomplished cooks—they inspire my belief that we've created a new generation of enthusiasts in the kitchen.

Index

About the Authors

TRACY, DANA, LORI, and CORKY POLLAN are the authors of the multiple award–winning cookbook, *The Pollan Family Table*. They are the recipients of the Global Green 2015 Sustainability in Food Award. The Pollans are *Huffington Post* contributors and write the monthly Pollan Family recipe newsletter.

TRACY has enjoyed a career on and off Broadway, in film, and on television. On Broadway, Tracy performed featured roles in Hugh Whitmore's *Pack of Lies* and Neil Simon's *Jake's Women*. Her film credits include *Promised Land* and *Bright Lights, Big City*. Notable television roles include the iconic comedy *Family Ties* and her Emmy award–nominated guest performance on *Law & Order: Special Victims Unit*. Tracy has served on the board of the Michael J. Fox Foundation for Parkinson's Research since 2000.

DANA has enjoyed an illustrious career in fitness, health, and nutrition. She cofounded the acclaimed Pollan-Austen Fitness Center, where she developed and taught innovative exercise programs and cocreated and appeared in a series of popular workout videos. Dana has made numerous appearances on television as a fitness and exercise expert. She has also been profiled and quoted extensively in prominent national magazines and newspapers, sharing her expertise on exercise, nutrition, and cooking.

LORI began her career in the health and fitness fields. She cofounded the renowned Pollan-Austen Fitness Center, where she developed and taught innovative exercise programs and cocreated a series of workout videos. Lori has consulted on and designed exercise, nutrition, and recipe features for innumerable magazines, television programs, and newspapers. She also blogs on wellness. Lori holds an MBA in marketing and is a certified life coach with a focus on health, wellness, and stress management.

CORKY has had a distinguished career in the magazine world. She was the editor of *New York* magazine's signature column, Best Bets, which she turned into the magazine's most popular column. Corky went on to become the style director of *Gourmet*, where she was involved in all aspects of the publication. She has written for the *New York Times*'s Dining Section and Well Blog, covered entertaining for *Coastal Living*, and is the author of *Shopping Manhattan*.